Praise for

MAKE AMERICA TALK AGAIN

"I've never been afraid of a few words—sticks and stones, right? Wise beyond his years, Brilyn Hollyhand's *Make America Talk Again* is about bringing back real, commonsense conversation in a country that's forgotten how to talk without losing its mind and trying to constantly cancel one another."

—**Kid Rock,** *multi-platinum recording artist*

"I know firsthand the importance of having tough conversations. It's something I make a point to do every day in the Senate, so I can deliver results for hardworking Alabamians, and it's a principle that must continue to be passed on to the next generation. That's why Brilyn's new book, *Make America Talk Again*, sparks an important call to action, challenging a new generation to speak up, think for themselves, and revive real conversation in America."

—**Katie Britt,** *US Senator (R-Alabama)*

"As a football coach, I know you can't build a winning team if nobody is willing to speak up in the locker room, and America's not that different. We need young patriots like Brilyn Hollyhand to carry on Charlie Kirk's legacy of speaking truth and help *Make America Talk Again.*"

—**Tommy Tuberville,** *US Senator (R-Alabama)*

"I know what it's like to be told to stay quiet for speaking the truth. Brilyn Hollyhand refuses to back down from the culture of intimidation, and *Make America Talk Again* is a rallying cry for anyone who believes truth is worth defending."

—**Riley Gaines**, *12x all-American swimmer*

"Washington is full of politicians who dodge tough conversations, and Brilyn Hollyhand runs straight toward them. In *Make America Talk Again*, he challenges Americans to stop shouting past each other and start fighting for the truth again."

—**Sean Spicer**, *former White House Press Secretary*

"I know championships aren't won by sitting on the bench; they're won by players willing to step up and lead. In *Make America Talk Again*, Brilyn Hollyhand is calling a new generation off the sidelines and onto the field of leadership."

—**Bruce Pearl**, *former head basketball coach at Auburn University*

"Brilyn Hollyhand's *Make America Talk Again* is a much-needed and powerful call to action for our time. Hollyhand is the bold and compelling voice for his generation with clarity and insight, encouraging readers to engage in the tough conversations our nation desperately needs in order to unite."

—**Barry Moore**, *US Congressman (R-Alabama)*

MAKE AMERICA TALK AGAIN

MAKE AMERICA TALK AGAIN

How to Save Humanity from a Screaming Culture

BRILYN HOLLYHAND

Since 1947
REGNERY
An Imprint of Skyhorse Publishing, Inc.

Regnery books may be purchased in bulk at special discounts for sales promotion, corporate gifts, fund-raising, or educational purposes. Special editions can also be created to specifications. For details, contact the Special Sales Department, Regnery, 307 Fifth Avenue, 4th Floor, New York, NY 10016 or info@skyhorsepublishing.com.

The author is represented by Tom Dean, Literary Agent with A Drop of Ink LLC, www.adropofink.pub.

Regnery® is an imprint of Skyhorse Publishing, Inc.®, a Delaware corporation. Visit our website at www.regnery.com.

10 9 8 7 6 5 4 3 2 1

Library of Congress Cataloging-in-Publication Data is available on file.

Cover design by David Ter-Avanesyan
Cover image by Molly Taylor

Print ISBN: 978-1-5107-8724-7
Ebook ISBN: 978-1-5107-8725-4

Printed in the United States of America

To Charlie Kirk

Like most kids in America, I grew up watching your videos. I never dreamed of the day I'd not only get to meet you, but also learn from you, and have you as a guest on my podcast. What I didn't know that day was that I had met my mentor, who would walk with me through my career, offer feedback after seeing me on TV, text me encouraging Bible verses, and strategize with me about my future. In a business surrounded by vipers, you were a true friend.

I keep trying and failing to wake up from this new world like it's some bad nightmare. On behalf of my entire generation that you practically raised, Charlie, thank you. This book is for you—to pick up where you finished your race. I hope it would have made you proud.

May your legacy be a long-term revival rooted in your courage for your faith.

*Then I heard the voice of the Lord saying, "Whom shall I send, and who will go for us?" And I said, "**Here am I. Send me!**"*

—Isaiah 6:8 (ESV)

Contents

Introduction

When people stop talking, really bad stuff starts. When marriages stop talking, divorce happens. When civilizations stop talking, civil war ensues. When you stop having a human connection with someone you disagree with, it becomes a lot easier to want to commit violence against that group. . . . What we as a culture have to get back to is being able to have a reasonable disagreement where violence is not an option.[1]

—Charlie Kirk

My college classmates have learned to write two versions of every paper: one they actually believe, and the "safe" one designed to please the activist in a professor's clothing lecturing from the front of the classroom. Friends tiptoe around honest conversations in the dining hall because disagreement now feels relationally fatal. Families avoid politics in the living room not because they lack convictions, but because they fear fracture. We "bite our tongues." We "don't want to offend." We "pick our battles."

Parents are intimidated. Teachers are warned. Students are graded down. Doctors are pressured. Pastors are neutered. Politicians are threatened. All for saying things that would have been uncontroversial a decade ago: Biology is real, truth matters, and feelings do not override reality.

Every time we make these choices to self-censor, the mob expands its territory. If they can successfully threaten us into silence by screaming at us from across the quad, unfollowing us on social media, moving away from us at the lunch table, and getting the classroom to turn against us, they're winning.

But courage has never been about applause or appeasement. It's about conviction. Turning Point USA founder Charlie Kirk lived that truth. He showed up on hostile campuses, stayed until every question was answered, and kept speaking long after it would have been easier to quit. The Left couldn't outwork him, so they tried to out-silence him. And that is the moment we're living in now.

Should each of us, looking at the problems of the world around us, grab a bullhorn and scream, dye our hair blue, get a nose ring, march in the streets, shut down a college campus, and burn American flags? Or do we do something a little bit more effective and a whole lot more rewarding? Get off our butts and work.

The idea for this book didn't come from an overpaid consultant, experienced speechwriter, or some polished marketing team. In fact, they all advised against it and said I had too much on my plate in my first semester in college.

The seed for this book was planted a few days after President Donald Trump was shot in a field in Pennsylvania. Then, when just more than a year later, my mentor, Charlie Kirk, was assassinated on a campus in Utah, the seed started to grow. That's why I decided to write the book you're holding. I couldn't take it anymore. The screaming. The hatred. The way disagreement stopped being something we debated and started being something we punished. It felt like the country I loved was forgetting how to talk, and when people stop talking, history shows they eventually start doing something far worse. This book is my attempt to push us back from that edge.

It all started when I was listening as Republican National Committee (RNC) staffers older than my parents went around during the strategy call, one by one, pitching themes for each night of the RNC's convention in July. Every idea was strong. "Make America Safe Again." "Make America Wealthy Again." "Make America Strong Again." They were tested, familiar, clean. They fit neatly on hats, signs, and bumper stickers. No one could argue with them.

Then it was my turn. Without overthinking it, I just said it: "Make America Talk Again."

There was a pause. Someone finally asked, "What does that even mean?" And in that moment, I realized I had been carrying the answer for a while. I remember saying that I thought it was the greatest problem of our time. That America hadn't lost its ability to shout—in fact, we had perfected that. We know how to scream at each other online. We know how to cancel. We know how to dehumanize. We even know how to assassinate someone we disagree with. What we have lost is the art of talking to one another, graciously disagreeing, and really listening.

America does not need a marketing department to endure. We simply need to start talking to each other again.

This book doesn't just need to be read by college students, parents, and grandparents who care about the future of America. It needs to be worn. It needs to be lived. If America is going to survive what's coming next, it won't be because we learned how to yell louder, click faster, or shoot straighter. Instead, it'll be because we remembered how to talk again.

America does not have a speech problem. We have a silence problem. We know how to shout. We know how to go viral. What we've lost is the willingness to talk honestly, courageously, and humanely. We've forgotten how to disagree without dehumanizing others. How to argue without annihilating. How to look someone in the eye across a table, be a bit angry or offended, and still pass the pie.

America does not have a speech problem. We have a silence problem.

Politicians, pastors, and pundits have spent years diagnosing what is broken in American culture. We have written books, hosted panels, posted threads, and argued endlessly about who is to blame. But an ivory tower diagnosis without the offer of a cure or any hope becomes just another talking point and a reason to unfollow someone. At some point, conversation has to move from analysis to action. And that point is now.

To my peers who are reading this, we all know the America we've been handed is not the same America that our parents and grandparents grew up in. And while we did not create the problem, it seems that all we have the courage to do is to complain. When are we going to do something? When are we going to refuse to tuck our tails between our legs and pretend to be liberal while writing an essay to get a better grade? When are we going to speak up in the dining hall when our friends beat up on America without biting our tongues to stay popular? When are we going to run for office instead of screaming at our current legislators?

I've never been a math guy—never have been, never will be. The truth is, once you walk out of your high school doors, you can probably live the rest of your life without touching algebra again. You might never write another essay or run another chemistry experiment. But there's one subject you don't get to opt out of: government. Whether you pay attention to it or not, it shapes your taxes, your freedoms, your opportunities, and the rules you live under every single day. You can ignore politics, but politics will never ignore you.

I don't believe in coincidences. I just don't. I don't know everything. I recently graduated from high school, for goodness' sake. But what I do know is these "God winks," these "random" moments of courage and hope that bring cultural transformation, are all part of God's plan. God put us here, in this country, right now, in its 250-year history, like he told Queen Esther, "for such a time as this."[1]

If you like hope and freedom, you should love America, because that is the whole point of this thing we call "the American experiment." If you like hope and freedom, how you live should matter. What you say should matter. What you do should matter.

I know what you're thinking. *Where do we start?* As simple as possible. Talking. That is why this book exists.

Talking is not yelling. Talking is not performative outrage. And the power of talking is highlighted well in Ronald Reagan's charge that "all great change in America begins at the dinner table."[2] But most importantly, talking is recognizing that even someone you believe is deeply wrong is made in the image of God and is deserving of dignity, patience, and kindness—and if you have the guts, maybe even a bit of conversation.

Charlie's warning that "When you stop having a human connection with someone you disagree with, it becomes a lot easier to want to commit violence against that group"[3] has become my assignment, and it is far more important than any work a professor might assign me.

Revival rarely begins in Congress, on cable news, or inside a university lecture hall. It begins when ordinary people decide to have the conversations the world tells them to avoid. It begins when someone becomes the first voice in a room full of silence.

---

1. Esther 4:14.

During my junior spring break in high school, I found myself boarding a plane headed south, farther than I had ever been from home, on a mission trip to Ecuador. At the time, I didn't fully understand why I felt such a pull to go. I just knew that something inside me said I needed to say yes. Not because it was easy or comfortable, but because obedience rarely is.

Ecuador was beautiful in a way that photos don't capture. The air was heavier, the colors sharper, the pace of life slower and more deliberate. We served in communities where basic needs weren't guaranteed, places where families worked hard just to make it through the week, and where faith wasn't discussed in abstract terms but lived out daily. We helped run a church camp, we served meals, and we listened more than we spoke. And for the first time, I realized how small my world had been and how big God's was.

One afternoon during the trip, standing in the middle of a dusty road surrounded by people whose language I barely spoke but whose humanity I deeply understood, familiar words from the Bible came to mind, this time with a clarity I had never experienced before: "Here am I. Send me!"[1] It was a moment of calling for me, or at least one in which I embraced my calling.

God wasn't asking for credentials or experience. He was asking for availability. For willingness. For a heart that would say "Yes" even before knowing the outcome.

That moment began to rewire something in me. I realized that God's call isn't limited by geography, age, or platform.

---

1. Isaiah 6:8.

The same God who sends missionaries across oceans is the God who sends young men and women into classrooms, corporations, campuses, and cultures that desperately need truth spoken with courage and grace. Ecuador didn't just teach me about service; it taught me about mission, that obedience often starts with stepping into the unknown, and that faith means moving before the path is fully lit.

When I came home, nothing about my surroundings had changed, but I had. I no longer saw my calling as something reserved for "someday" or "someone else." I understood that if I could say "Here am I" in Ecuador, I had no excuse to avoid saying it back home in the Bible Belt. In my school. In my family. In my work. In my generation. In a culture increasingly hostile to truth but starving for meaning. The ends of the earth weren't just overseas; they were right in front of me.

That trip didn't give me all the answers, but it gave me something better: a conviction that my life is not meant to be spent avoiding discomfort or chasing applause, but responding, again and again, to the same simple question God has been asking for thousands of years: "Whom shall I send?" And every time I've stepped forward since then, whether onto a stage, into a debate, or into a moment that required courage, I've carried Ecuador, and the quiet roar of God, with me.

Every one of us has a sphere of influence, a classroom, a workplace, a friend group, a dinner table. And those places become battlegrounds when truth grows unpopular. The question is not whether you have influence. The question is whether you will use it to protect your comfort zone or fulfill your calling.

Jesus, the greatest man who ever lived, loved well, challenged hypocrisy, gave dignity to women and children in a time and place that overlooked them, and saved us from ourselves. He showed us the path forward, and He made sense of the past. He did many things—in fact, so many that one of the biographers of Jesus recorded in the Bible that "This is the disciple who testifies to these things and who wrote them down. We know that his testimony is true. Jesus did many other things as well. If every one of them were written down, I suppose that even the whole world would not have room for the books that would be written."[1]

But one thing Jesus never did was allow neutrality. He spoke to Matthew the tax collector and Simon the violent extremist, men who should have been enemies, and told them to follow Him.[2] Jesus was at work doing what He saw His Father in heaven doing. But it was up to Matthew and Simon to choose to join Him. The same is true of you and me.

You see, to make a difference in the world, we have to discover, embrace, and live in the truth. And today, the truth is that most people just refuse to talk to each other anymore.

Conversations have become combative. We are afraid of debating ideas with friends and family because it will be awkward, and we might learn we are wrong, or worse, get canceled. Our fear is making us lonely while, at the same time, making us louder than ever. To overcome this, we have

1. John 21:24–25.
2. See Matthew 9:9–13; 10:4.

to have the courage to be unimpressive, to just be ourselves. We have to muster the humility to listen and learn. And if, in the end, we think the other person is so wrong that it makes our heads spin, we should be able to disagree well, say "Please" and "Thank You," shake hands, and go our separate ways. And we really, really need to stop screaming.

In the coming pages, I want to introduce (or remind) you to the wisdom of the American Founders, the wit of some of my favorite critics, and the words of leaders who care about you, me, and civil discourse. You'll read about my experiences as a college student in America, not so you can watch me live, but so you can learn a little bit more about the phenomenon that is Cultural Marxism (that devious, self-serving power grab rooted in the lie of "systemic inequality") and how its foothold in academia is spreading to every part of America. And throughout it all, I want to keep pointing you toward courage. Courage for truth. Courage for conviction. Courage for conversation. And I want to encourage you to consider the value of what Charlie said when he was asked how he wants to be remembered: "I want to be remembered for courage for my faith."[4]

On one of his final radio broadcasts, Rush Limbaugh, the godfather of conservative talk radio, delivered a message that felt less like commentary and more like a charge to the country he loved. Battling cancer and fully aware his time behind the microphone was coming to an end, he told his audience something simple but defiant: "It is never going to be time to panic . . . because we're not going to give up on America."[5] Rush reminded listeners that the American story has always been written by people who refused to surrender to decline. Empires fade when citizens lose faith in themselves, but America survives when ordinary people choose to stand up, speak out, and defend the ideals that built it. Even in one of his final moments on the air, Rush didn't sound defeated. He sounded determined. His message was clear—as long as Americans still believe in this country and are willing to fight for it, the story of America isn't over. It's still being written.

Rush understood something many people today have forgotten: America doesn't collapse because people disagree. America collapses when people stop talking to each other altogether.

> ***If America is going to survive, we have to learn how to talk again.***

If America is going to survive, we have to learn how to talk again. Not perform. Not posture. Not scream. Talk. That is what this book is about. And that is where we begin.

PART I
WHAT WE LOST

Chapter 1
When Conversation Became Combat

Every difference of opinion is not a difference of principle.[1]

—Thomas Jefferson

Americans are not silent because we have nothing to say. Instead, we stay silent because we've been indoctrinated to believe speech is dangerous.

We don't suffer from a lack of speech in the technical sense. We are surrounded by words, flooded with noise, and drowning in opinions that never seem to shut off. Every screen is filled with commentary, every timeline moves at a pace no human was designed to process, and yet beneath it all, there is a growing quiet that should terrify us. Not the quiet of peace or reflection, but the quiet of hesitation—the quiet of people who know what they want to say but have learned, often the hard way, that saying it out loud comes with consequences they are not sure they can afford. We didn't lose our voices overnight; we surrendered them one awkward moment at a time. This is the silence that defines our moment.

It is the silence at the dinner table when politics come up, and everyone pretends they are suddenly very interested in passing the cornbread. It is the silence in classrooms when a professor makes a sweeping claim and students stare at their notebooks, not because they agree, but because they know disagreement will cost them. It is the silence in offices when coworkers exchange glances that say, "Don't go there," because they have all seen what happens to the person who does. It is the silence online when people watch lies spread unchecked and tell themselves it is wiser to stay out of it.

We are told this silence is maturity. We are told it is strategic. We are told it is the price of living in a pluralistic society. But none of that is true. This silence is not wisdom. It is fear that has learned how to sound reasonable. And fear, no matter how politely dressed, always produces rotten fruit. Silence doesn't protect you; it delays the moment you'll be forced to speak without preparation. And this default position toward silence comes to us, I think, because we all subconsciously agree with the sentiment of Mark Twain: "We like a man to come right out and say what he thinks, if we agree with him."[2]

During this past spring semester, I committed to speaking at ten universities' Turning Point USA chapters, and everybody around me told me how dangerous it was: my family, my friends, and my security team. All I kept hearing from everybody was, "You can still cancel," "Nobody will blame you for staying home," and "Have you lost your mind?" I'll be honest, the severity of it didn't sink in until the first stop at the University of Arkansas, when armed campus police met me on the tarmac to sneak me past the protesters and into the lecture hall.

All the stops went off without a hitch. They all had protestors. A few drew pretty chalk pictures of my head getting blown up, others held kindly worded signs telling me "You're next" with a picture of my assassinated friend, and some got in line at Q&As to debate why I hurt their LGBTQIA+ friends' feelings. And none of it got to me until Clemson University.

It was already a super chaotic campus stop. I had an exam that morning, a grilling interview with the *New York Times*, and a not-so-flattering photoshoot with *New York Magazine*. So, by the time I waited outside the door to walk into the lecture hall and do the Clemson stop, I was exhausted and still had a speech, Q&A, meet and greet, and 8:00 a.m. class the next day ahead of me.

The speech went off without a hitch. I could hear some protestors outside, but they used their bullhorns, and I used my inside voice and had conversations while they screamed obscenities. After I started the Q&A, we got to a student who wanted to talk about one of the hot-button issues on the news that day. As we both respectfully went back and forth, after I answered one of his follow-ups, I paused to turn to the audience and said, "Look! We both disagree, but what we're doing is called civil discourse. Adults should try it sometime. He hasn't screamed or shot me." And just at that moment, he stood up and said, "Well, not yet." I remember security looking over at me and motioning to the door, but I shook my head. When the audience quieted down from their gasps, I took the next question.

People who stay quiet today don't avoid conflict tomorrow; they inherit a worse tomorrow with fewer options and higher costs. Martin Luther King Jr. wrote from the Birmingham Jail, "We will have to repent in this generation not merely for the hateful words and actions of the bad people but for the appalling silence of the good people."[3] This sentiment alone dismantles one of the most comforting lies we tell ourselves—that staying quiet is somehow morally neutral. History doesn't fall apart because evil suddenly becomes persuasive or intelligent. It falls apart because ordinary, decent people convince themselves that speaking is dangerous, impolite, or not worth the cost. Silence does not pause injustice. It participates in it. It allows lies to harden into norms and corruption to settle into institutions without resistance. And that is precisely why silence has always been tyranny's most reliable accomplice: it looks reasonable, sounds mature, and feels safe, right up until the consequences arrive.

President Ronald Reagan understood this erosion at a generational level. In his inaugural address as California governor, he warned Americans that freedom is never automatically passed down from one generation to the next; it must be "fought for, protected, and handed on,"[4] or else it disappears quietly while people assume someone else will defend it. Reagan wasn't predicting tanks rolling down Main Street. He was diagnosing complacency, just like King was in that jail cell—the slow decay that happens when people mistake peace for permanence. Freedom doesn't usually collapse in a dramatic moment. It fades when citizens grow silent, distracted, and comfortable, only realizing what they've lost after they've forgotten how to defend it, kind of like understanding and defining what it means to be a woman.

Scripture does not treat words lightly because words are never neutral. From the beginning, God created with speech. He brought order out of chaos by His spoken word. Light exists because it is spoken into existence. And throughout the rest of Scripture, words mark the dividing line between obedience and rebellion, courage and cowardice, faith and fear. The Book of Proverbs in the Bible is blunt because the author, King Solomon, understood human nature better than most modern psychologists ever will. Death and life are in the power of the tongue, not because words float in the air disconnected from reality, but because words shape the direction of our lives long before actions ever do.

Silence Is Not Safe

Safety has become the god of modern America. We worship comfort, bow to approval, and sacrifice truth on the altar of not being bothered. And then we act shocked when lies move faster than truth.

You don't have to explain to me that speaking out is scary. I've lived it in ways most people hopefully never will. I've had strangers send me photos of my own house, letting me know they knew where I slept. I've received messages describing what they'd do to me if they ever got the chance—not abstract threats, but detailed ones, written with the kind of confidence that makes your stomach drop. I've been sitting in class, trying to focus on a lecture, only to realize someone across the room is watching me, whispering, recording, posting. I've been out to dinner with friends and felt my phone vibrate with messages from strangers telling me they know where I'm eating. I've walked downtown with people I love and had cars slow down, just to scream my name out the window, to remind me I'm not welcome, turning a regular night into a reminder that my anonymity is gone. I've had people jump up and scream at campus events, security stepping in while my heart raced. I've had others wait by my car afterward, just to make sure I heard what they thought of me.

I've lost friends who decided proximity to controversy wasn't worth it. I've watched conversations stop when I sat down at a dining hall table, felt eyes follow me, and felt the quiet calculation of whether associating with me would cost someone socially. I've lost followers, opportunities, and invitations, not because I was cruel or dishonest, but because I refused to be quiet. And I'm not telling you this for sympathy. I'm telling you because fear doesn't disappear when you choose courage; it just loses its authority.

Trust me, walking on your own campus with armed men in suits around you isn't the rockstar life you dream of as a kid. It's the real-life result of speaking out.

I walked into the gym not too long ago after a particularly controversial day. One of those days where you turn on the TV and see your own name getting ripped apart by people who have never met you. My face was literally on the screen on the wall while I was walking in. But I was smiling. Someone looked at me and asked how I could possibly be in a good mood after a day like that. I told them something simple: God woke me up today. I've got breath in my lungs, Jesus in my heart, and I'm living the dream of getting to inspire people for a living. When you look at life that way, through the lens of gratitude, criticism doesn't scare you. It just reminds you that what you're doing actually matters.

Silence would have been easier. Retreat would have been safer. But if the cost of speaking is isolation, intimidation, discomfort, or fraud, the cost of silence is far worse. Because once you train yourself to stay quiet to survive, you don't just give up your voice; you give up a piece of who you are.

Violence Unleashed

A generation that refuses to speak will not suddenly find its courage when it matters most. Look at this moment in history: our silence isn't just enabling bad ideas; it is creating a moral fog where violence is becoming explainable and even expected. In recent years, political violence in America has been rebranded through euphemisms. Just take a look at this headline from the *New York Times*: "We'll See You at Your House."[5] Planned attacks that are celebrated by allies are described as "isolated incidents." Perpetrators are framed as "troubled individuals." And people who commit crimes are called "bad actors."

This rhetorical softening matters. When violence becomes explainable, it becomes repeatable. When natural law and moral clarity are replaced with humanist and Marxist worldviews, no matter the political party, excuses replace accountability. A society that refuses to draw hard lines invites more violence, not because people suddenly become more violent, but because boundaries stop existing. Sadly, an October 2025 poll found that 30 percent of respondents agreed with the statement, "Americans may have to resort to violence to get the country back on track." And before you roll your eyes at "the other team," the percentages by political party affiliation were 28 percent of Democrats, 31 percent of Republicans, and 25 percent of Independents.[6]

Political disagreement does not require moral hatred. But when opponents are dehumanized long enough, someone will eventually take the rhetoric literally.

I knew we lived in a fallen world, but it never really hit me until Charlie Kirk's assassination last year. It wasn't even the assassination itself that made it sink in; it was the reaction. I was off my phone for a while after I got the news, and that night, when I couldn't sleep, I opened social media, expecting to see unity and tributes to my slain friend. Instead, I saw people I sit in class with, people who teach me, family friends I grew up with, taking a victory lap and posting celebratory messages like "karma" in response to the gruesome video we all can't get out of our heads.

How did we get to this point in our country where violent attacks aren't only normalized, but people are so numb that they feel the need to rejoice because the murdered victim had an "R" beside his name?

There was a time in America when political opponents still recognized each other as human beings. When President John

F. Kennedy was assassinated, reporters went into deeply conservative Dallas neighborhoods and spoke with Republican women who had voted against him, criticized him, and feared his policies. And what did they find? Tears. Real grief. These women weren't celebrating a political victory; they were mourning a murdered president, a widowed wife, and fatherless children. They understood that bullets aren't ballots, and assassination isn't a substitute for elections. Now look at where we are. When Donald Trump was shot, parts of the internet didn't respond with horror. In fact, they responded with applause. Jokes. Memes. Celebration. People openly wishing the shooter had better aim. That isn't just political disagreement; that's moral decay on full display. It reveals how far we've fallen from a country that argued fiercely but mourned together into a culture where some would rather see their opponent dead than defeated. A nation cannot survive when compassion becomes partisan and violence becomes entertainment.

America now treats political violence as tragic but acceptable, depending on who the victim is. What makes this moment especially dangerous is how subtly silence has been sold to us as safety. Nobody is holding a gun to your head and demanding that you shut up. Instead, you are offered incentives. Keep quiet and keep your job. Keep quiet and keep your GPA. Keep quiet and keep your reputation. Keep quiet and keep your friends. Keep quiet and avoid being dragged into a

> ***America now treats political violence as tragic but understandable, depending on who the victim is.***

public fight you never asked for. Over time, the calculation becomes automatic. You stop asking whether something is true and start asking whether it is worth saying. That shift changes everything.

Once speech becomes a cost-benefit analysis, truth becomes optional, and courage becomes reckless rather than virtuous. Eventually, people begin to believe that the highest good is not honesty, but not rocking the boat. That is how free societies decay, unnoticed until it is too late.

At some point, a society—and, more importantly, the individuals who live in it—has to decide whether it values truth more than trends, and courage more than applause. In the last few years, we have failed that test. We have replaced honesty with euphemisms and traded natural and moral reality for social approval. So, let's stop dancing around it and call it what it is.

- A man can never be a woman.
- Cultural Marxism is devastating humanity.
- Voluntary abortions are murder.
- Climate change activism is about controlling behavior.
- Human nature is inherently evil.
- Porn is destroying women, men, girls, and boys.
- Social media makes bullying easier.
- Politicians are complicit in widespread financial fraud.
- Christianity produces the highest form of human flourishing.
- DEI is the opposite of freedom.
- Islam is not compatible with Americanism.
- LGBTQIA+ is a mental illness, not a birth defect.

To say any of these things in public is to risk violence, harm, and now, even death. To say these things makes someone else a "victim of your hatred." And the problem with that? It seems that, in America today, victimhood is the most popular identity because it excuses inaction. It demeans humanity. It prevents individuals from helping their neighbors. Worst of all, it isolates people from hope.

Still, it is time to start talking to each other so the truth can be revealed and political violence can be eradicated instead of celebrated in the streets with guillotines. Guillotines, you say, Brilyn? Surely you exaggerate. Nope. During a protest against US Immigration and Customs Enforcement (ICE) operations in Asheville, North Carolina, protestors got inspiration from the evils of the French Revolution and raised a guillotine with the words "NO KINGS DE-ICER" scribbled on it.[7] Cardboard as it was, its symbolism is not lost on those who know the evils of secular-humanist history and the Marxists who repeat it.

What makes this moment especially dangerous is not just the lie itself, but the enforced silence around it. And here's the part no one wants to admit: the Left didn't stumble into this. They built it. They weaponized empathy, reframed dissent as violence, and taught an entire generation that disagreement is harm. The result is coercion, not tolerance. This isn't freedom, but fear. And this won't bring us healing; it will bring us silence. "Who are they?" you ask. I hate to be a guy who quotes his own writing, but here it goes, from my book *One Generation Away*:

> Who are they? Allow me to distinguish *they* from *them*. They are the anti-American Marxists who congregate

> on the very left edge of the Democratic Party. They are not Democrats in the tradition of John F. Kennedy, but rather anti-God elitists who are passionately pro-human evolution while being ardently anti-baby. They are progressives, meaning that they want America and its values to progress as far away from our founding as quickly as possible, no matter where it goes.
>
> But they are not them. Them are our Democrat colleagues on the other side of the aisle. Them are pro-freedom liberals who are part of the Democratic Party for one reason or another. Them are your parents and grandparents who have always voted for government support nets, union interests, and the funding of public schools.
>
> I don't have a problem with them. I have a problem with the Left, which makes up the they who find their home in the Democratic Party.[7]

Why am I concerned? Because the Marxists and their anti-God friends have gained so much ground in the last century. And they don't talk about the concerns of everyday people; they scream at you and me, informing us that our ideas of God and science and country and constitutional rights are racist. They lie to blue-collar workers who are convinced that their hard-earned money, taxed by the government, is being spent to house, feed, and support illegal immigrants in a quiet (and illegal) exchange for votes. They conjure talking points and marches to create civil unrest to make us feel afraid of our neighbors, so under the guise of safety, we give them the power they want so they "can protect us." They lie that masks work to stop the spread and vaccines make it impossible to get the virus. They lie and tell conservatives, both young and old, to sit down, shut up, and buy what they are selling. And this is all happening now, in every facet of American society, because it first happened in our universities.

Violence Indoctrinated

I've seen this play out on college campuses firsthand. Professors push gender ideology harder than they push critical thinking. Students whisper concerns like confessions. Parents are shut out of life-altering decisions. And when someone finally speaks up, they're told to sit down, shut up, and "trust the experts," even as those same experts refuse debate and punish dissent.

> ***A society that cannot question its own dogmas is not enlightened. It is fragile.***

A society that cannot question its own dogmas is not enlightened. It is fragile. For example, if we actually cared about people struggling with gender dysphoria, we would invest in mental health support, long-term counseling, and honest conversations, not lifelong medical dependency. We would protect children from irreversible harm, not recruit them into it. We would treat distress as a signal for help, not an identity to be celebrated.

But that would require courage. And courage is in short supply.

Calling something a mental illness is not a condemnation. It is the first step toward treatment. Toward hope. Toward healing. And the longer we refuse to say it out loud, the more damage we do—not just to individuals, but to families, institutions, and the moral credibility of an entire culture.

I'm not saying this; doctors said this for decades until they were threatened and told they could not say this anymore.[8]

In the eyes of the alphabet mafia, humans can re-create themselves into whatever sex they want to be. It does not matter how God made you; you can decide if you are a man or a woman. But "transsexualism" was not a rational notion to anyone who has seen a man or a woman naked, never mind those who have an understanding of humanity made in the image of God. Thus, the word was replaced with another to make it more ambiguous and acceptable. And then the obvious natural disorder was made even more confusing when it was replaced with "dysphoria." And then it was decided it wasn't even a mental disorder at all.

Ideas matter. Truth matters. How we handle this, and other equally important issues, matters. And yes, there's a right way and a wrong way.

Responding to the Violence

I can't count the number of times a day I hear some version of the same advice, always delivered with a knowing tone, as if it's wisdom passed down from a calmer, wiser generation: "Turn off the news." "Don't engage." "Protect your peace." "Cover your ears and focus on your own life." And

I understand the impulse. The world is loud, angry, and exhausting. But here's the problem: That advice only works if you don't care what happens next. Silence doesn't diminish the noise; it hands the microphone to someone else.

While decent people log off to preserve their sanity, activists don't rest. Ideologues don't unplug. Radicals don't "take a break." They organize, they indoctrinate, and they fill the vacuum left behind. Telling a generation to disengage in a moment like this isn't self-care. It's surrender. History didn't move forward because good people stayed informed in private. It moved when they spoke out in public, even when it was uncomfortable or cost them something. You don't defend a country and the truth it is founded on by tuning it out; you defend it by standing in the noise and refusing to be quiet.

Silence may be comfortable. But comfort is not compassion. Comfort has replaced courage, and everyone wonders why things feel broken.

In the early 1930s, Germany did not descend into Nazi horror overnight. In the beginning, there were no mass arrests, no camps, no gas chambers. There were laws. Bureaucracy. Incremental shifts that felt technical and mundane. Jewish professionals were quietly removed from positions. Independent newspapers were regulated, then folded. Speech wasn't originally banned outright; it was discouraged, stigmatized, and eventually punished selectively. Most citizens did not cheer these changes. They simply watched them happen.

What made this moment uniquely dangerous was not fanaticism, but normalization. Neighbors told themselves politics was not their responsibility. Church leaders focused inward, choosing quiet preservation over public confrontation. Business owners stayed silent to protect their livelihoods. Each decision felt rational, even moral, until those isolated silences fused into national paralysis. By the time opposition became unavoidable, it was no longer possible.

History does not remember the good people of Germany for their lack of information. It remembers them for their lack of resistance. Evil advanced not because everyone agreed, but because too many people decided disagreement was too costly.

Most Americans know something is wrong today, even if they cannot articulate it. According to a Sine Institute poll in October 2025, when asked to respond to the question "How would you describe the situation with regard to civil discourse in the U.S. today?" 28 percent indicated we are in "a crisis," 41 percent called it "a serious problem," and 26 percent identified the current state of civil discourse as being a "somewhat problem." Friends, that is 95 percent. I don't know of anything in America that we agree on 95 percent of the time! Yet, these same respondents indicated they believe "respect," "open-mindedness," "empathy," and "active listening" are the solutions to the problem. These outpace their preference for "self-awareness," "humility," "patience," "tolerance," "curiosity," and "courage."[9] As for me? I'd put my money on "self-awareness," "humility," "patience," and "courage" as the answers to the problem.

Because of competing worldviews, the most prominent in America being the proclamations of the Bible and the claims of Cultural Marxism (that is, the application of Marxist theory to social and cultural issues, presented as solutions to perceived problems of inequality), we often cannot agree on why something is wrong, why it is happening, or what to do about it. The default response is to blame politics, technology, or the media, and while all of those play a role, none is the root of the problem. I believe the deeper issue is that we have trained ourselves to believe that silence is the responsible choice. It is not.

Every authoritarian system in history thrived not because most people agreed with it, but because most people decided it wasn't worth the trouble to object.

Silence does not protect institutions. It hollows them out. Silence does not preserve relationships. It turns them shallow and transactional. Silence does not prevent conflict. It postpones it until it explodes in uglier, more destructive ways. When people stop talking, they do not stop disagreeing. They stop trusting.

Every authoritarian system in history thrived not because most people agreed with it, but because most people decided it wasn't worth the trouble to object.

I saw this dynamic long before I knew what to call it. One of my first real speaking opportunities came when I was still in high school and was invited to speak to college students at the University of Alabama at Birmingham (UAB). By any standard, I did not belong there. I had never navigated campus life. I did not know what pressures college students faced day to day. I was still figuring out how to stand behind a podium without feeling awkward. Everything about that invitation screamed that it would be safer to say no.

But safety has a way of shrinking your life—if you let it.

I showed up anyway. And when it was time to speak, only one student walked into the room. One. I could have treated it like a joke. I could have rushed through my remarks and moved on, telling myself it did not matter. Instead, I gave the speech I prepared. I answered his questions. I spoke as if the room were full. Two days later, I spoke at another school. That moment did not feel significant at the time, but looking back, it revealed something fundamental about how courage actually works. It does not wait for ideal conditions. It does not require validation. It moves forward even when the outcome feels uncertain.

Silence would have been easier. It would have been safer. I could have learned to stay quiet. Some say I should have.

That is the trap silence sets. It convinces you that nothing is lost by staying quiet, when the greatest losses are the ones you never see because they never happen. The conversations you never have. The people you never reach. The callings you never step into because you decided it was safer to stay where you were.

This mindset has now been institutionalized, especially on college campuses. Look around. Higher education has quietly transformed from arenas of debate into zones of risk management. Don't believe me? I watched my friend be assassinated at one of these "places of free expression" for trying to express his views freely.

The shift didn't happen through official bans on speech; it happened through incentives. Students learned quickly which opinions triggered consequences and which earned approval. Conservative and religious students weren't expelled; they were conditioned. They learned to phrase essays carefully, to avoid certain topics entirely, and to read professors' politics before raising a hand. The result is not education but self-surveillance. When students graduate having mastered silence rather than argument, they don't enter adulthood prepared for anything, never mind leading. Instead, they enter it trained to comply. This is how the Left is fighting against America today. This is their preferred method of combat.

During my first semester of college, I finished a ten-stop campus tour.[10] Different schools, different states, different political climates, but the same pattern emerged every single time. Before students asked about elections or policy or the economy, they asked one question: "How do I survive college as a conservative?"

That question alone tells you everything you need to know about the environment they are in. Survival is the language of captivity, not education. Students are not asking how to think better or argue more clearly. They are asking how to avoid being targeted. How to keep their heads down. How to make it through four years without becoming a problem.

That is not because they lack conviction. It is because they have learned the rules.

Students have told me they avoid entire majors because they know disagreement will be punished. They avoid conversations with fellow students who self-identify as liberal activists because they know, if something goes wrong, whose side the administration will be on. They avoid displaying the American flag in their dorm rooms even though they have one in their bedroom at home.

Silence has become a survival mechanism. But survival is not the same thing as freedom. And a generation trained to survive instead of speak will eventually inherit a country that reflects that choice.

> ***Silence has become a survival mechanism. But survival is not the same thing as freedom.***

Thinking back to the respondents in the poll conducted by the Sine Institute, when they suggested the answers to civil discourse are "respect," "open-mindedness," "empathy," and "active listening," I want to suggest a different answer. I want to tell you, and them (if any of them are reading this), what the Bible says about civil discourse—not in a sermon, but in a practical lesson for humanity.

In the New Testament of the Bible—the part that begins with the Gospels of Mathew, Mark, Luke, and John—about the life and teachings of Jesus, there are more than fifty commands given to humanity about how we should live with one another. Appropriately so, many Christians refer to these Bible verses as the "One anothers" of the Bible. Often written by a follower of Jesus who was caring for the people in a nearby church at the time, these verses explain how we should *love* one another, live at *peace* with one another, be *kind* to one another, *serve* one another, and *teach and encourage* one another. A few of my favorites are "Honor one another above yourselves,"[1] "Let us not become conceited, provoking and envying each other,"[2] and "Spur one another on toward love and good deeds."[3]

The reason for this book and the call to "make America talk again" is not because I think we have a political problem (which we obviously do), but because I believe we have a human problem. It seems to me that, for whatever reason, and however it happened, we forgot how to be human. We forgot how to live in the way that the Bible says is the ultimate way to live, with "love, joy, peace, patience, kindness, goodness, faithfulness, gentleness, and self-control."[4]

If we are to save our friendships, our families, our workplaces, our schools, our cities, and our country, we have to start talking to each other once again. We have to learn the value of speaking with each other, sharing ideas, and debating worldviews. We have to risk offending others and being offended ourselves. We have to take stock of the risk and talk anyway. Humanity depends on it.

1. Romans 12:10.
2. Galatians 5:26.
3. Hebrews 10:24.
4. Galatians 5:22–23.

CHAPTER 2
The Awkward Death of Conversation

A candle loses nothing when it lights another candle.
—Benjamin Franklin

The most efficient form of control is the kind that convinces you that it is your idea. And the easiest way to control people is to convince them they're powerless. Make them afraid. Tell them they should be scared. Take away their power. That is a recipe for tyranny.

In today's America, silence isn't just a personal choice; it's a national trend with measurable consequences. According to research from *Time*, "1 in 2 adults are estranged from a close relative. While the primary cause of these rifts is often tied to something a relative said or did, 1 in 5 directly cite political differences as the reason."[1] What makes this silence, which is directly connected to an unwillingness to talk with each other, so effective is that it rarely announces itself as intimidation. It presents itself as personal care and protection, emotional intelligence, or social awareness. I wonder how often these lines of thinking are used to justify selfish behavior and not, as the Bible commands, "Be patient, bearing with each another in love."[1]

You are told that speaking up is unnecessary because "everyone already knows," or it is irresponsible because "this isn't the time," or it is selfish because "there are bigger issues."

The language is always soft. The pressure is not. Over time, people internalize the message that truth is something to be managed rather than expressed and that conviction is a liability rather than a virtue. And they stop talking about anything and everything.

This is how fear becomes structural. It does not rely on constant enforcement. It teaches people to enforce it on themselves, kind of like what we did with masking during the COVID-19 pandemic.

Once that happens, institutions do not need to silence dissenters because dissenters silence themselves. Administrators do not need to issue warnings because students already know the consequences. Employers do not need to fire people to make a point because the threat alone keeps everyone in line. The most efficient form of control is

1. Ephesians 4:32.

the kind that convinces you that it is your idea. And the easiest way to control people is to convince them they're powerless. Make them afraid. Tell them they should be scared. Take away their power. That is a recipe for tyranny.

That is why silence is so contagious. When people see others punished for speaking, they do not need to experience it personally to learn the lesson. Fear is observational. It watches. It adapts. It tells you to take notes. And the cost of resisting that fear feels higher the longer you wait.

I watch this play out repeatedly on campus, not just in what students say, but in how they say it. Their eyes scan the room. Their voices drop when they talk about faith or politics. They ask questions that begin with apologies: "I don't want to sound crazy, but . . ." "I'm probably wrong, but . . ." "I know I'm not supposed to say this, but . . ." And they avoid conversations with "the wrong people." This preemptive self-flagellation is not humility; it is armor. It is how they protect themselves from a system that has taught them honesty comes with punishment.

This did not start with my generation, but it has accelerated with us. We grew up watching people get dragged online for a sentence taken out of context, lose jobs over tweets from their childhood, and become permanent villains wearing tinfoil hats for holding the wrong view at the wrong time—such as vaccinating babies may be harmful to their health, or chopping off kids' genitals will harm them in the long run. We learned early that silence is safer than clarity and that ambiguity is a shield.

What can be done about this, individually and culturally?

Death of Awkwardness

Revolution rarely looks the way people expect it to. We imagine marches, megaphones, dramatic speeches, and sweeping moments that feel cinematic in hindsight. But most cultural change does not begin with spectacle. It begins with discomfort. With moments that feel clumsy, socially risky, and deeply uncool at the time they happen. Awkwardness is not a sign that something is wrong. More often, it is evidence that something real is happening.

Our generation has been trained to fear awkwardness more than almost anything else. Awkwardness means you misread the room. It means talking on the phone. It means you said something that did not land. It means the group chat goes quiet. It means you feel exposed without the protection of applause or outrage. It means making eye contact in a job interview. In a culture obsessed with smoothness and polish, awkwardness feels like failure. But I am arguing that awkwardness is often the birthplace of courage. Remember my speech to one person?

Awkwardness is the first crack in the wall of conformity. The regime of silence survives by convincing you that speaking up is socially fatal, until one person does it anyway. Every cultural shift begins with someone willing to make a room uncomfortable. Comfort preserves systems. Discomfort changes them.

Boomers love to quote the line, "Strong men create good times, good times create weak men, weak men create hard times,"[2] usually as a warning aimed squarely at younger generations. What they rarely do is pause long enough to ask where they fit into that cycle. Because the uncomfortable truth is (boy, this is awkward), many of the people now lamenting decline were the ones who presided over it. They inherited a nation built on sacrifice, discipline, faith, and shared moral expectations, and slowly traded those things for comfort, convenience, and cultural surrender. They didn't lose America overnight; they managed it gently downward, one compromise at a time, until stability turned into stagnation and conviction turned into apathy.

And now, as the consequences finally arrive, a new generation is being forged under pressure. Gen Z didn't grow up in good times; we grew up watching institutions fail, prices soar, families fracture, and truth get treated like an inconvenience. That kind of environment initially creates confusion, but when we talk through the problems, it creates clarity.

I like the history documented in the Bible and the many leaders it records (as both good and bad examples of leadership) under the watch of a faithful God. One such story is that of Joshua. He stepped into leadership after Moses, facing unknown territory, hostile opposition, and responsibility he did not ask for. God did not tell him to be impressive. He told him to be strong and courageous. God did not promise ease. He promised presence. God challenged Joshua as he stepped onto the stage: "Have I not commanded you? Be strong and courageous. Do not be afraid; do not be discouraged, for the Lord your God will be with you wherever you go."[1] Now, some Christians will use this as a totem, believing that whatever they do, God will bless. But mature (that is, not foolish) Christians understand that when we

1. Joshua 1:9.

walk in faith and do the right thing, God will be with us and he will be pleased. That distinction matters. Courage is not confidence that everything will work out. It is obedience despite uncertainty. And obedience is rarely socially comfortable.

Os Guinness once wrote that "faithfulness, not effectiveness, is the biblical measure of success."[3] This is a truth that cuts directly against modern instincts. Effectiveness is measurable. Faithfulness is costly. One earns applause; the other often earns isolation. But history does not move because people were efficient. It moves because someone stayed obedient when results were uncertain and affirmation was absent. Awkward obedience has always been the spark of real change.

Mahatma Gandhi understood this same tension when he insisted that "in matters of conscience, the law of the majority has no place."[4] Truth does not wait for consensus. Conscience does not take polls. Courage acts when the time comes.

Waiting until speaking feels socially safe is not wisdom; it is surrender disguised as patience.

> ***Waiting until speaking feels socially safe is not wisdom; it is surrender disguised as patience.***

Embracing Your Awkward Influence

Almost every breakthrough begins with someone willing to be uncomfortable. Someone trying something for the first time. Many of us can remember the moment we yelled, "Hey, Dad, look at me!" right before a fall that caused others to laugh.

Awkwardness is what happens when you stop performing and start acting. It is the pause in conversation after you say something true that disrupts the script everyone else was following. It is the silence that follows a question no one wanted asked. It is the feeling of standing slightly out of sync with the room. That feeling is not danger itself. It is resistance. And it can be really good.

If honesty feels awkward, it's usually because lies have been normalized. Every system relies on predictability. Social norms, institutional habits, and cultural scripts all function because people know how to play their part. Awkwardness disrupts that predictability. It forces recalibration. It exposes assumptions. It slows the moment down long enough for truth to enter. That is why awkward courage is revolutionary. It breaks patterns.

I have seen this repeatedly, especially among young people who assume they need to be perfectly prepared before they speak. They wait for the right phrasing, the right tone, the right moment. They wait for everything to be just so, so they will be liked no matter what they do. But as former British prime minister Margaret Thatcher warned, "If you just set out to be liked, you would be prepared to compromise on anything at any time, and you would achieve nothing."[5] The right moment rarely arrives wrapped in confidence. It arrives wrapped in nerves, uncertainty, and the nagging feeling that maybe you should just stay quiet. That feeling is the threshold. And to embrace your influence and actually accomplish something, you need to step over it and walk through it, especially when it comes to talking to people.

Now, what I am saying here is nothing new. Books have been written on courage and leadership. Sermons have been preached on how to talk to your spouse with love and respect. And parents have had to sit their kids down and force them to talk about their problems, helping them find the words and emotions to express how they feel. I don't want to be new. I just want to awkwardly use my twenty years of life to teach someone something they need to know. But I do so, not from a place of authority, but a place of awkward curiosity, because as C. S. Lewis said in *Mere Christianity*,

> Really great moral teachers never do introduce new moralities: it is quacks and cranks who do that. As Dr. Johnson [a contemporary of Lewis] said, 'People need to be reminded more often than they need to be instructed.' The real job of every moral teacher is to keep bringing us back, time after time. To the old simple principles which we are all so anxious not to see. . . .[6]

I know that you know what it feels like to be in the middle of an awkward moment. I know you remember overcoming your stage fright and mumbling your way through a speech in middle school. Or the time you ended an interview by courageously asking for the job. Or shared your thoughts on Donald Trump with a member of your family. Well done! Those awkward moments are part of the same principles of courage that we are all anxious to avoid. I think most people initially step back from these moments because they interpret discomfort as a warning sign. (I know I sure have, and still do.) But courage helps us interpret discomfort differently. Courage recognizes that awkwardness is often the price of integrity. You are not awkward because you are wrong. In fact, you are awkward because you are no longer playing along.

The Comfort of Comfort

I believe one reason we avoid awkward moments is that our culture has elevated comfort to the highest good. We optimize ourselves and our circumstances for smooth interactions, frictionless experiences, and unchallengeable identities. Anything that threatens us is disregarded as rude, offensive, immoral, impolite, or irresponsible. But this line of thinking, this dismissive thought process, is a tool of control—by us, yes, but also by those who seek to divide and control us. And awkwardness is what happens when we refuse to be controlled.

The early stages of courage are rarely impressive. They are often quiet, unseen, and socially costly in small ways that add up. A raised hand in a classroom. A question asked when everyone else wants to move on. A refusal to repeat a talking point you do not believe. A calm disagreement in a room that expects silence or applause. These moments feel awkward because they violate expectations. But that violation is precisely what makes them powerful. They remind people that consensus is often fragile and that conformity is not the same as conviction.

Awkward courage also reveals who is actually listening. When a room goes quiet, it is tempting to assume you have failed. More often, you have forced people to think. Silence is not always rejection. Sometimes it is processing. Sometimes it is a relief that someone finally said what others were afraid to articulate.

The problem is that we rarely give those moments time to work. We rush to fill the silence. We apologize unnecessarily. We backpedal. We reframe in ways that undo the disruption we just created. In doing so, we train ourselves to retreat from the very moments that could change the trajectory of a conversation.

> ***Awkwardness is only dangerous if you flee it in pursuit of comfort.***

How big a deal is it to pursue comfort at the expense of something else? Enough that someone wrote a book called *The Comfort Crisis*. And there is a quote often attributed to Marcus Aurelius that says, "Comfort is the worst addiction," and a quick Google search of the terms "comfort addiction" returns articles and blogs with the following titles:

- "Is 'Comfort Addiction' Real?"—*Psychology Today*
- "How to Breath the American Addiction to Comfort"—Outside 365
- "Comfort Is the Worst Addiction, and It's Costing You More than You Think"—LinkedIn
- "Are We Addicted to Comfort?"—Heal Your Health Now

People are asking these questions. And we should. But we should also have the courage to put aside our demand for safety and comfort and walk—awkwardly, if necessary—into moments that demand our attention.

When assuming his leadership role, Joshua did not step into leadership with a flawless plan or universal support. He stepped into uncertainty with obedience. That obedience required him to endure discomfort, resistance, and moments of doubt. It required him to move before everything felt settled. That pattern repeats throughout Scripture because it reflects how change actually happens. God does not wait for perfect conditions. He works through imperfect people willing to act without guarantees. And if imperfect people are good enough for God to work with, maybe we should let Him work though us as well. And how do we do that? By being willing to have awkward courage.

Awkward Courage

Awkward courage is the modern expression of that ancient truth. It looks small. It feels uncomfortable. It rarely earns applause. But it creates cracks in systems that depend on silence and performance. It risks reputation and relationships. It is willing to encounter a sleepless night of second-guessing. It means speaking up even when it's uncomfortable. It means having the courage to post the truth online when you know you'll face backlash. It means defending your faith in a classroom where your professor rolls his eyes. It means telling the truth about America, even when the culture insists you stay quiet. Every time we speak, we take ground. Every time we refuse to back down, we keep alive the legacy Charlie gave us. Awkward courage embodies what Mark Twain describes as, "Courage is resistance to fear, mastery of fear, not absence of fear."[7]

Awkwardness is going to happen. You can't avoid it. It happens when you say the wrong thing, act the wrong way, or let your guard down for a moment. It is losing a game in the first round. It is having someone forget your name (or worse, forgetting someone else's). It is avoiding eye contact with someone you know you disappointed. But awkward courage is still thanking Jesus for the ability to play the game even though you lost. Apologizing to someone for not remembering and starting the relationship over. Saying I'm sorry and believing you are forgiven.

Now, what I am not encouraging you to do is to be socially awkward, especially at school and work. There are many good and meaningful social behaviors that we should all be aware of and practice as often as we can: a few come to mind:

1. Make eye contact during conversation, but don't stare.
2. Don't be sarcastic in meaningful conversations.
3. Don't give one-word answers.
4. Don't stand too close to people, especially when debating.
5. Stay in the moment. Pay attention. Listen.
6. Be kind and gracious when receiving a compliment.
7. Know when it is time to end a conversation.
8. Don't keep talking when a movie, class, or meeting is about to start.
9. Don't involve yourself in conversations that don't involve you.
10. Avoid dark humor and crude jokes. Always.

We can learn a lot from our parents' and grandparents' generations. While they also struggled with pride and a desire to pretend that they were better than they were (or not as worse off), they had decorum. There was a time when people did not mock southern manners. There was a time when kids didn't talk rudely to their parents or their elders in general. Or at least it was known to be classless to do so. It wasn't long ago that "Yes, ma'am," and "No, sir," were spoken by people of all ages. If we want to save ourselves from the screaming, maybe we can be the ones who start saying "Please" and "Thank you" again, as awkward as it might be in our self-centered age. I have the courage to do so. Do you?

You see, awkward courage threatens the status quo. It makes people look at you, and then themselves. And in that moment, when awkwardness interrupts instinct, the hardened systems built on compliance begin to lose control. This is why social pressure from ruling classes, sycophants, hard-hearted religious leaders, abusive bosses, and others who demand submission (especially the Left in America) escalates so quickly after someone breaks script. The first response is often confusion. The second is correction, shaming, or public rebuke. And if correction fails, punishment follows. Most people comply at that stage—not because they agree, but because they are uncomfortable being uncomfortable.

Social pressure is subtle when it works best. It comes through tone, facial expressions, side conversations, and unspoken signals. You feel it when the room shifts and the temperature drops. You sense it when people avoid eye contact or change the subject too quickly. No one has to say anything directly. The message is understood. This is not how we do things here.

Awkward courage resists that message by refusing to rush past the moment. It does not escalate. It does not apologize for existing. It allows the discomfort to sit long enough to do its work, to cause people to start looking at themselves.

Have you ever felt out of place? Maybe you were the smallest person on the football team, the youngest person at the table, or the newest (and least informed) member of a planning committee. Right before the 2024 presidential election, I Zoomed in to give a speech at Harvard University after one of my classes one afternoon. I was in my senior year of high school staring down graduation, and there I was, engaged in conversation with Ivy League students. Sure, I didn't fit in; I'm a "conservative" from the South. I'd barely started enrolling in my college classes, and most of them were not relevant to our discussions. But I went. I could have said no. I could have decided I was not ready. But I went, with awkward courage, and I met with students who I assumed, rightly so, would disagree with my ideas about God, country, and family. And it was amazing! No one screamed. We talked and listened. We honored one another. And while I stand by my comments saying, "I'm all in on President Donald Trump's bold move to consider yanking $9 billion in federal funding from Harvard University for its complete failure to address the rise of antisemitism on campus,"[8] I can't wait to go back to pick up the conversation where we left off.

The Awkward Conversation

Still, institutions of all types fear this kind of disruption because it cannot be easily managed. Loud protests can be contained. Outrage can be dismissed. Awkwardness, especially when calm and consistent, is harder to neutralize. It does not provide a villain. It does not escalate into spectacle. It simply refuses to comply and invites others to join the dissent.

That refusal is why awkward courage feels revolutionary. It does not announce itself as rebellion. It operates within the system while quietly challenging its assumptions. The irony is that awkward courage often looks unimpressive in the moment. There are no cheers. There is no validation. Sometimes there is not even a response. But its impact accumulates. It reshapes expectations. It alters what feels possible. And over time, it changes the environment in ways that loud gestures never could.

This is especially important for people who do not see themselves as activists or leaders. You do not need a platform to practice awkward courage. You need proximity. You need relationships. You need the willingness to risk mild discomfort for the sake of integrity. That willingness, repeated over time, is far more disruptive than a single dramatic act.

Awkward courage also exposes the limits of performative tolerance. Many environments pride themselves on openness and inclusion until someone actually tests those claims. The moment a belief outside the accepted framework is expressed, the response reveals whether tolerance is genuine or conditional. Awkwardness forces that revelation. It draws a line between values that are stated and values that are practiced.

A 2024 survey by Public Religion Research Institute (PRRI) found that about 65 percent of Gen Z teens share their parents' party affiliation, showing that young people are politically aligned and deeply socialized into ideological identities, yet more than half of Gen Z teens and young adults identify as independents or with "other/don't know," signaling a pattern of disillusionment and non-traditional identification.[9] At the same time, other research points to younger generations being more individualistic and reactionary with their moral frameworks, viewing politics through personal ethics rather than social obligation. These trends underscore the complex way young people approach political participation—not with passivity, but with a mix of skepticism, identity fluidity, and ideological openness.

To the Gen Xers and Boomers who are reading this, it seems to me that many of my peers are willing to join the conversation, but much like Millennials, we have been dismissed and disregarded. Maybe we are like other generations, and we are "just kids." But we are willing to listen, so long as you hear us out as well. We are willing to learn from the past, so long as you don't just tell us what to do. We are the most technologically savvy and informed generation, knowing many things about way too much that is going on around the world, even as we hold all the same ignorance that prior generations did when they were young. We know we will be the youngest people at the table, and maybe even the least informed, but we are willing to show up. At least those of us who are willing to stop screaming long enough to offer a firm handshake, look you in the eye, listen first, and then talk. I know there are seats open because some of your peers have already given up and left the room.

You have the power to keep the conversation going. Give us a seat, will you? No matter how awkward it might be.

The Awkward Fight

This chapter is not a call to speak constantly or impulsively. It is a call to stop treating discomfort as disqualification. Feeling awkward does not mean you made a mistake. It often means you are standing at the edge of growth. Avoiding that edge guarantees stagnation.

Revolution does not require perfection. It requires participation. Awkward courage invites ordinary people into extraordinary impact by asking them to do something very small and very hard: show up honestly where you are.

I have watched rooms change simply because someone stayed. The first time they spoke, it was awkward. The second time, it was tolerated. The third time, it was expected. Eventually, it became normal. Nothing dramatic happened. No confrontation, no spectacle. Just steady presence and consistent honesty. That is how norms shift.

There is a fight going on, and it is a fight for the soul of America. And while there have been protests in the streets, yet again, it is not a battle against racism or immigration enforcement or any other distraction that the Left throws at us. It is a fight for courage, and it is a battle for ideas—chiefly, the definition of truth.

A society that cannot articulate what it believes will eventually be ruled by those who are willing to say anything loudly enough. When reasonable people withdraw, extremists fill the vacuum. When moderates go quiet, radicals set the terms of debate. Silence does not de-escalate conflict. It hands power to the loudest and least restrained voices in the room.

This is why outrage thrives in a culture of fear. Shouting feels safer than talking because shouting does not require vulnerability. It does not require listening. It does not risk being persuaded. It simply overwhelms. And in an environment where persuasion is dangerous, volume becomes a substitute for truth.

But shouting and silence are not opposites. They are partners. Both avoid the hard work of conversation. Both flatten human beings into caricatures. Both refuse to engage the image of God in the person across from you. One withdraws. The other attacks. I take very seriously a caution offered in the Bible: "My dear brothers and sisters, take note of this: Everyone should be quick to listen, slow to speak and slow to become angry, because human anger does not produce the righteousness that God desires,"[1] which is why I want to talk and not scream.

Talking, real talking, requires something far more demanding. It requires you to believe that truth exists and that people are capable of recognizing it, even if they resist it at first. It requires patience. It requires discipline. It requires the willingness to be misunderstood without becoming bitter. That kind of courage is not rewarded by algorithms or applause. It is cultivated slowly, often in hostile environments, often at personal cost.

That cost is not theoretical. It is awkward. It is scary. It is paralyzing. And it ruins reputations and relationships.

During my campus tour in 2025, every single stop came with threats. Some were vague enough to be brushed off.

1. James 1:19–20.

Others were detailed enough to make me stop and reread them twice. By the end of the tour, my security team placed a binder in front of me, thick with flagged messages. Thousands of them. Promises of violence. Promises of silence enforced permanently.

I remember stepping out of the room, away from everyone else, and asking God why this was happening. I remember wondering what my life would look like if I put the microphone down and chose a quieter path. I could have gone back to being a normal student, going to class, doing homework, living a life that stayed safely within the lines. Nobody would have blamed me. Most people would have understood.

This moment reminded me of my flight back from Ecuador, where I had gone on a mission trip with my church. During that flight, because of the overwhelming joy I had in serving God, I wondered if I should become a missionary. People need to hear about Jesus's love for them and the truth about the world they live in, and I could do that. On the flight, I reflected on the verse that had come to mind on that dusty road, "Here am I. Send me."[1] What did God want me to do? I enjoyed my podcast and debating ideas. I was fascinated by what I was learning from my "mentors" as I listened to Rush Limbaugh and Ronald Reagan. Should my future be in the church or outside of it? With a bit of conviction and a quiet nudge from God, before the plane landed back in the United States, I decided I wanted to share the light of Christ in the darkness of American politics. Can you think of a darker arena?

---

1. Isaiah 6:8.

Back on campus, having talked a bit more with God about my future, I awkwardly walked back into the room and told my family and security team that the tour was continuing. That same afternoon, at nineteen years old, I drafted plans for what would happen if someone decided to make good on their threats. That is not a detail I share for shock value. It is a reality check. When you choose to speak in a culture that punishes honesty, you are forced to decide what you are willing to lose.

When I think of "awkward," it is not just about tripping in front of a girl you like or forgetting someone's name. It's not just the look you get from your friends when you take a full swing, and the golf ball bounces twenty yards from the tee box and into the water. Awkward also occurs the first time you talk about writing a will, or hear your name called, joined by a frantic invitation to walk on stage. It is the uncomfortable bats flapping their wings in your stomach the first time you try something new. For example, drafting my plans for what I wanted to see happen if someone killed me was awkward. It could have been prevented by an honest, uncomfortable, embarrassing, and real conversation.

Here is the part that confuses people: The idea of someone killing me does not scare me the way it probably should. I do not say that flippantly. I remember the night my friend Charlie died. I remember pacing in the early hours of the morning, after my phone finally stopped ringing, collapsing onto the floor, and begging God to give him back. I had talked to him the day before. He had been a mentor, a friend, a steady voice in an industry full of vipers.

The following week, I stood on another campus holding a microphone, looking out at a crowd of students, and the thought crossed my mind that I could be next. And what surprised me was not fear, but peace. The worst a coward can do is refuse to debate me or shoot me from a rooftop. One leads to intellectual bankruptcy. The other leads me out of a broken world and into eternity with my Creator. I could die quietly at the age of one hundred, or I could die somewhere between now and then on the front lines of something that actually matters. I know which one I choose.

That peace did not come from recklessness. It came from clarity. When you settle the question of who you serve, fear loses its leverage, so long as you have the courage to speak the truth to God, to yourself, and to others.

Again, a free society depends on citizens who are willing to articulate what they believe and why they believe it. They don't have to do it perfectly, but honestly. And not aggressively, but with humility. When that willingness disappears, power does not lose its grip; it tightens it. Values, through public policy and peer pressure and unspoken incentives, still rule the day; it is just that the rulers are the ones who were willing to speak, and the quiet ones are no longer allowed to debate openly.

The tragedy is that many people participating in this silence believe they are being loving. They think withholding the truth is kindness. They think avoiding disagreement is humility. They think peace is found in keeping conversations shallow and safe.

That is why silence feels virtuous in the short term but is devastating in the long run. It allows false ideas to harden unchallenged. It allows institutions to drift without accountability. It allows leaders to mistake compliance for consensus. And it leaves ordinary people feeling powerless, wondering how everything became so distorted so quickly.

How did we get here? How did we devolve from a country with two major political parties to two countries defined by opposing political viewpoints? How did the killing of an unborn baby become celebrated, the taking of wages to buy votes from illegal aliens become standard practice, and when did everyone start screaming at each other?

The answer is simpler than we like to admit: We stopped talking. We must start talking again. Not screaming. Not posting. Not performing outrage. Talking. The kind of talking that requires listening. The kind that assumes the person across from you is more than an enemy avatar. The kind that refuses to surrender truth while still respecting human dignity. That form of conversation is costly, and it is precisely because it is costly that it matters.

Talking forces clarity. It exposes weak arguments and strengthens good ones. It builds resilience in the speaker and discernment in the listener. It creates the conditions for persuasion, which is the only legitimate way ideas are meant to spread in a free society. Coercion can enforce behavior, but it cannot command belief. Silence may postpone conflict, but it guarantees decay.

This is why the lie of safety through silence is so dangerous and why we need to have awkward courage. A people afraid to speak will never defend themselves when it counts. They will wait for someone else to do it for them, and by the time they realize no one is coming, the cost will be far higher than it ever was at the beginning.

Every generation faces this test in its own way. Ours just happens to be facing it earlier and more intensely than others in the past. Social pressure now operates at the speed of the internet. Punishment is public, amplified, and permanent. The instinct to retreat is understandable. But understandable does not mean justified.

If you have a pulse, you have a purpose. That is not motivational fluff. It is theological reality. God does not create people accidentally or place them in history randomly. The same God who called young men and women into impossible situations throughout Scripture still does so today. Peter stepped out of the boat before he knew how it would end. David ran toward Goliath without armor or guarantees. Esther risked her life by speaking when silence would have preserved her comfort. None of them was called because they were safe. They were called because they were willing.

That willingness is what our moment demands.

Death and life are in the power of the tongue because speech reveals allegiance. Every time you choose silence out of fear, you are making a declaration about what, and who, matters most. Every time you choose to speak with clarity and conviction, you are doing the same. Those choices compound. They shape character. They shape culture. They shape the future.

I've already mentioned how Joshua's leadership began, and now I want to be sure you know how it ended. Following many battles and great hardships, and many opportunities to give up on God and join pagan societies in worshiping their false god, the people of Israel had a choice to make, and Joshua made it clear:

> Now fear the Lord and serve him with all faithfulness. Throw away the gods your ancestors worshiped beyond the Euphrates River and in Egypt, and serve the Lord. But if serving the Lord seems undesirable to you, then choose for yourselves this day whom you will serve, whether the gods your ancestors served beyond the Euphrates, or the gods of the Amorites, in whose land you are living. But as for me and my household, we will serve the Lord.[1]

Every day is a time for choosing. Every conversation is an opportunity to profess your courage and faith. Silence is not safety. Awkward is not the end of your life. Conversation isn't that scary. But it is the first step toward saving our friendships, family relationships, communities, and courage.

---

1. Joshua 24:14–15.

Chapter 3
Platforms over People

Let us not be blind to our differences, but . . . direct attention to our common interests.[1]

—John F. Kennedy

Every generation has its favorite idol. Not the kind carved out of stone, but the kind that quietly rearranges priorities and reshapes behavior without asking permission. For some generations, it was power. For others, it was money. For Gen Z, it is applause. Not applause in the obvious sense of standing ovations or packed arenas, but the constant, low-grade craving for affirmation that now governs how people think, speak, and act. Things like likes, shares, retweets, follower counts, trending topics, and approval from the right people in the right rooms. We track validation the way earlier generations tracked savings accounts. And like any addiction, it always demands more.

Look at what we're swimming in every day. Movies out of Hollywood push the line a little further every year. Teen shows that used to be about high school drama now feel like soft-core shock value. Scroll your social media timeline, and it's the same story—algorithms feed hypersexualized content because outrage and lust both keep people hooked. None of this happens by accident. When a culture normalizes pornographic imagery and treats intimacy like entertainment, it chips away at the very things that hold communities together: self-control, respect, commitment, and the ability to see other people as human beings instead of objects.

You can't rebuild a culture of strong families, real relationships, and honest conversations with your neighbors while the dominant message everywhere else is instant gratification and public exhibition. A society that constantly trains its eyes on voyeurism shouldn't be surprised when it loses its appetite for virtue—or its patience for civil dialogue. If we want a country that talks again instead of tearing itself apart, we can't ignore the cultural pipeline that's quietly eroding the moral foundation underneath it.

This is the hidden engine behind much of our cultural dysfunction. We are not just afraid of speaking. We are afraid of honest conversation. We are afraid of not being liked. We are afraid of being ignored. We are afraid of being on the wrong side of whatever the room decides is acceptable. Silence often feels safer than rejection, but receiving applause feels even safer than silence. An entire generation has been trained to perform their socially accepted (if not made-up) beliefs in public to avoid being canceled.

This problem of talking more than we listen, wildly expressing our opinions so we can validate ourselves, and pursuing righteous indignation is not a Left vs. Right problem; it is a moral problem. It is affecting friendships and families. It is ruining conversations and communities. And it has definitely made it so people love or hate politics because this new era of "angertainment" is feeding our selfish, sinful desires to be praised by some while feeling good about righteously hating others.

One of my first videos to reach the million views threshold was reacting to this loud, liberal influencer around my age named Harry Sisson. That started what the internet labeled as a rivalry, where we've responded to each other's videos and Tweets for the last few years. You'll even see us debate on TV from time to time. What you don't see are the texts exchanged offline.

It started on Election Day 2024, of all days. It was one of the most hectic days of my life, and I remember walking into one of the last events of the day and finding Harry on TV, celebrating what he expected to be the day former vice president Kamala Harris made history.

I remember laughing and taking out my phone to type the following text:

> Harry, just wanted to say it's been a fun campaign and I hope our paths cross again! So glad to have so many energetic first-time voters on both sides of the aisle! Best of luck tonight!

When I walked out of the event, I found his reply to be,

> At the end of the day, the betterment of our country comes before anything else. I appreciate the message and good luck tonight, Brilyn!

It is possible for me to disagree with every single argument Harry makes, and fiercely debate him on TV in an effort to persuade people away from his ideas and toward the truth, but at the end of the day, we can still have conversations. We're both humans, and we're both Americans.

The media demands that we be enemies with our opponents, and that has contributed to where we are today. People don't know how to talk to the other side because they're not friends with anybody they disagree with. They've isolated themselves on an island with like-minded friends, and that's as dangerous as it gets. You don't know your opponent's arguments, you aren't experienced in defending yours, and you're both just talking in echo chambers. I don't think Harry and I will be playing golf anytime soon, but we'll continue to be friends because that's what America is about.

As you are probably aware, there is a great deal of tension in America about the role of the Supreme Court and the apparent biases of the justices. One side blasts the "Trump conservatives." The other side demeans the "liberal justices." Given the rhetoric outside the courtroom, you'd think that these nine judges would all be watching their backs at every turn, with their "sworn enemies" just a few seats away. But that is clearly not the case. I appreciate the kind words of Christopher Scalia about the friendship between his dad, the conservative late Supreme Court justice Antonin Scalia, and the liberal late Supreme Court justice Ruth Bader Ginsburg:

> With the passing of Justice Ruth Bader Ginsburg, many people wonder how she and my father, the late Justice Antonin Scalia, managed to be such good friends despite having such different views about the law.
>
> It seems so unlikely to some people that they ask me bluntly, "I hear they were friends—is that true?"
>
> Yes, it is . . .
>
> Judge Jeffrey Sutton, one of my father's former clerks, tells a story about visiting my father at the Supreme Court on what happened to be Justice Ginsburg's birthday. My dad had bought his old friend two dozen roses for the occasion, and Judge Sutton started teasing him, joking that there was no point to a gift like that when Justice Ginsburg had never sided with him in an important 5-4 case.
>
> My father replied, "Some things are more important than votes."
>
> The point of this story isn't that my father or Justice Ginsburg changed their votes to please the other, or that they pulled any punches when writing differing opinions—indeed, they are both known for their strong dissents. The point is that they didn't let those differing and deeply held convictions undermine their dear friendship.[2]

Every movement eventually faces a test that has nothing to do with elections and everything to do with character. For the conservative movement, that test is unfolding right now, and we should all learn from Justice Scalia. There is a small but loud faction on the Right that mistakes outrage for courage and cruelty for conviction. They believe shock value is strength and that winning arguments matter less than humiliating opponents. They call themselves bold. In reality, they are brittle, incapable of persuasion, addicted to attention, and dangerously unserious about the moral responsibility that comes with influence. Now, everyone should be welcome to work out their thinking, in public, awkwardly, and imperfectly. But when a person persists in rage-baiting or pursuing clicks, or forces evil ideas into the marketplace masquerading as truth, there needs to be a discussion about the discussion. At the time of my writing, people like Nick Fuentes and his useful idiot trolls have been expressing rhetoric that is not fit for these pages. From praising certain facets of Islam and Naziism to telling you to never marry or have kids because you need to focus more on your jawline and body count, these voices, while they have the right to exist, are not advancing healthy conversation. While it has not been this way in the past for every influencer entertaining this degeneracy, right now, all are talking more than they are listening, sharing wild ideas that have little or no merit but get good click rates, and expressing indignation about how they think things are going. This is not helping America thrive.

Today, a small faction of influencers with radical ideas seems more interested in burning bridges than building arguments, more focused on shock and likes than persuasion and earning votes, and more addicted to attention than conviction. These are the personalities who tell young voters not to participate in elections, who flirt with extremist rhetoric just to provoke outrage, and who treat politics like a livestreamed cage match instead of the serious responsibility of governing a country. Their business model isn't persuasion. It's provocation. And unfortunately, that behavior is finding far too much comfort under the "big tent" of the Republican Party. If we sit on our hands and allow the mainstreaming of people fantasizing about rape, idolizing Joseph Stalin, and proudly saying they're "team Hitler,"[3] we won't just lose every election going forward by legitimizing the Left's lie that we're Hitler Juniors. Instead, we will lose the moral war that conservatives are supposed to uphold.

We have seen this movie before. A decade ago, the Democratic Party dismissed its most radical voices as "fringe." In the 2016 Democratic presidential primary, voters were overwhelmingly in favor of Senator Bernie Sanders from Vermont, a Democratic Socialist. But he was too much for the party at that time. While some would argue that this was just a power play of the Clintons, Washington, DC insiders of that era generally agreed that Sanders and his voters were too extreme to matter and too unserious to shape the party. But instead of confronting them, leadership indulged them. That fringe became the base. And the base now defines the party, and socialists like Representative Alexandria Ocasio-Cortez from New York (AOC) and New York City Mayor Zohran Mamdani are their leading voices; they are called "passionate," "energizing," and "the future."[4]

A Letter to My Fellow Republicans

> ***You can be a bold conservative without being a bitter one.***

To my fellow Republicans, you can be a bold conservative without being a bitter one. You can stand with me and say we send no money overseas until our debt hits zero. You can call out alleged corruption within lobbyist groups or the Israeli government without blaming "the Jews" for every minor inconvenience in your life. You can demand secure borders and a merit-based immigration system that puts Americans first without shutting the door to legal immigrants who want to join the workforce and build a better life. You can fight corruption without dehumanizing entire groups of people. You can criticize institutions without embracing hatred. You can reject globalism, fight for secure borders, and defend national sovereignty without surrendering moral clarity. Conservatism was never meant to be defined by who we despise, but by what we defend: Faith. Family. Freedom. Ordered liberty.

You can be unapologetic without being unhinged. When rhetoric turns cruel, we don't win converts; we confirm caricatures of ourselves. And when we excuse it all in the name of "fighting back," we lose something more valuable than elections: credibility.

The Democratic Party of John F. Kennedy didn't collapse and get swallowed up by the Leftist movement in America because it debated too much. It collapsed because it replaced reason with rage. If we allow the same instincts to take root in the Republican Party, we won't lead a movement; we'll manage its implosion.

When a movement abandons those principles in favor of perpetual outrage or constant applause, it loses the ground that made it worth defending in the first place. Winning elections means nothing if the victory requires sacrificing the very values we claim to protect.

We do not need a woke Right that is addicted to applause and virtue signaling, just as the Left is. We need a sane Right more than ever, grounded, disciplined, and confident enough to win without becoming what we oppose.

Nearly three thousand years ago, God gave humanity a warning, one that we should pay attention to now. It was spoken to the Prophet Isaiah, and it was intended for the people of Israel, but it reveals a great deal of the heart of God for all of humanity.

> Wash yourselves; make yourselves clean;
> remove the evil of your deeds from before my eyes;
> cease to do evil,
> learn to do good;
> seek justice,
> correct oppression;
> bring justice to the fatherless,
> plead the widow's cause.
>
> "Come now, let us reason together, says the Lord:
> though your sins are like scarlet,
> they shall be as white as snow;
> though they are red like crimson,

they shall become like wool.
If you are willing and obedient,
you shall eat the good of the land;
but if you refuse and rebel,
you shall be eaten by the sword;
for the mouth of the Lord has spoken."[1]

We have been created and invited to join in reason, with God and each other. These words from God act as a guide for every person, whether they are a Christian or not, Republican, Democrat, or Independent. God is prioritizing people. He is telling Israel, and us, that we should seek the good of others, uphold righteousness, and eradicate evil in our own lives and in our communities. We need to not only pay attention to the plight of others; we need to do something about it. We can do this through our families. We can do this as members of our church and synagogue communities. And we can do this through our governments. And we should.

A Test

Some moments stop you cold, not because they make sense, but because they remind you how little control you actually have over the path God sets in front of you. I had just finished a Fox News appearance and was hustling across campus to make my morning class, backpack slung over one shoulder, still half-thinking about what I should've phrased differently on air. It was one of those ordinary college mornings, students rushing by, earbuds in, heads down, everyone living

1. Isaiah 1:16–20, ESV.

in their own little bubble. Then my phone buzzed. One text. Five words: "Trump just posted about you."

I stopped walking.

Sure enough, there it was, a clip from Fox, my commentary playing on Truth Social, shared by the president of the United States.[5] The leader of the free world, apparently sipping his morning Diet Coke, had decided to repost a few minutes of something I said. I stood there on the sidewalk staring at my screen, pinching myself like a cartoon character, and quietly muttered, "God . . . how?"

My platform was growing. I could hear the applause. And with applause comes temptation. Not the kind most people think of, but the quiet pressure to become the version of yourself that the algorithm rewards. I remember staring at my phone one night after a clip of mine started going viral. The comments were pouring in, the numbers were climbing, and I knew exactly what kind of response would make it explode even more. All I had to do was sharpen the edges a little more, be a little nastier, a little more sarcastic, a little more outrageous. The internet rewards that version of you. It turns politics into a performance and disagreement into a spectacle.

But I also knew something else: if I started chasing applause instead of truth, I'd eventually become the same kind of voice I criticize—loud, angry, and addicted to attention. I could rack up views that way, but I would lose something far more important: the ability to actually persuade people who disagreed with me. So I put the phone down. Because the goal isn't to win the algorithm. The goal is to win hearts and minds.

How does an eleven-year-old kid who started a fourth-grade newsletter, recording interviews from his bedroom with a cheap microphone and seven subscribers, most of them family, end up in a moment like this? How does someone who used to nervously ask teachers if he could miss class to appear on a radio show now see his words amplified to millions with the tap of a finger?

And yet, as surreal as it felt, the moment wasn't about validation. It was about responsibility. Platforms aren't prizes. They're tests. They ask a simple question: What are you going to do with the microphone once it's handed to you? It reminded me that influence isn't proof of correctness, and visibility isn't permission to coast. If anything, it's a heavier weight. Because when words travel further, they matter more.

That morning didn't make me feel bigger. It made the calling feel heavier and clearer. If God could take a kid with a conviction, a willingness to speak, and a refusal to stay quiet, and put him in rooms and moments like that, then the only faithful response is to keep saying what's true, even when it's uncomfortable, even when it costs something. Especially then.

Catechism and the Culture of Performance

What or who disciples you shapes what you defend and what you're willing to say out loud. TikTok has catechized Gen Z more effectively than most churches and schools combined.

The culture of approval and punishment is measurable. A recent Pew Research Center survey found that 61 percent of US adults say they have heard a fair amount or a great deal about "cancel culture," up significantly from 44 percent just a few years prior, showing how widespread the concept has become across age and ideological groups.[6] Young adults, especially ages eighteen to twenty-nine, are particularly familiar with the term, and about 55 percent of voters aged eighteen to thirty-four report having participated in canceling a public figure or company for offensive content online.[7] Notably, opinions are mixed: While many see these behaviors as accountability, others view them as unfair punishment. "Nearly half of respondents, 49%, said they believe cancel culture has had a negative effect on society, while 27% said they think it has had a positive impact."[8] These numbers reveal how the pursuit of applause and fear of backlash are embedded in public discourse beyond any single demographic or platform.

This addiction did not start with social media, but social media perfected it. Platforms designed to connect people now function as real-time approval meters. You know immediately whether what you said was celebrated or punished. You learn, through repetition, which opinions earn affirmation and which earn backlash. Over time, this feedback loop reshapes behavior. People stop asking what is true and start asking what will land well. They adjust tone, language, and even beliefs to fit the expectations of the crowd.

That shift happens gradually, almost invisibly. Few people wake up and decide to abandon their convictions. Instead, they soften edges here, avoid topics there, and adopt language that signals alignment without requiring substance. They convince themselves they are being strategic or compassionate. In reality, they are being trained. Applause is a powerful teacher.

Modern media no longer just reports events. Instead, it dictates acceptable emotions. If you consume information via any news outlet, you should know what the editorial intent is behind their efforts. This is the reality. This is the world we live in. We are told what we already believe so we keep watching. Confirmation bias keeps us staring at ourselves and those we agree with. The tech and media giants know this, and their algorithms are designed to keep giving us more and more sugary cereal when we really should be eating a salad. And the scary part? Freedom doesn't disappear overnight; it erodes while people scroll.

Maybe it has always been this way, but it is especially true in our Attention Economy, and, specifically, in our digital environments where attention is currency. Need an example? Now that X is monetized, in a similar fashion to YouTube, shocking and outrageous posts earn more money than moderate, faithful, integrity-filled posts.

This is where the culture of performance, that innate desire to meet the expectations of others and gain their approval and applause, collides directly with the call to reason. Reasoning requires patience. It requires coherence. It requires the willingness to lose applause in the short term for the sake of credibility in the long term. Applause culture cannot tolerate that delay. It demands immediate payoff. If an argument does not land instantly, it is discarded. If a position requires explanation, it is dismissed as weak. Complexity is punished because it slows the cycle of validation. The result is a politics of constant emotional spikes and shallow convictions.

You can see this play out in how quickly positions shift depending on the audience. People speak one way online and another way in private. They adopt different vocabularies for different rooms. They learn how to signal belonging without committing to substance. This is not because people are inherently dishonest. It is because the cost of consistency has been artificially inflated.

I've lost count of how many times I've walked into rooms where I was clearly the youngest person there, sometimes by decades. People with resumes longer than my life, grandkids older than me, titles that carried weight, white hair, and wisdom that I have not yet earned. And I learned quickly that age doesn't intimidate people as much as clarity does.

I'll be honest, it did at the beginning. It got to me. Made me get a lump in my throat when every boardroom, fundraiser, or strategy session was filled with people older than my Granny and Paw Paw. But I vividly remember the first time I spoke up.

It was in the Reagan Conference Room of the Republican National Committee headquarters in Washington, DC. We were discussing how to get the 2020 presidential primary debates in front of younger audiences. I had a yellow legal pad in front of me that I had grabbed at the hotel and scribbled down an idea on the walk over: "streaming."

I shared with them that our party had been in an echo chamber for too long. I was talking about the year-after-year efforts broadcasting debates on conservative-friendly networks, posting on conservative-run social media sites, and speaking at conservative-heavy campuses. What if we broke the mold? What if we approached this nontraditional election in a nonrational way? What if we aired all the primary debates on the same sites my classmates went to watch their favorite video game streamers?[9]

The Grand Old Party agreed. They were finally modernizing with the times, and I got to be a part of it. The strangest thing happens when you speak with conviction: people stop seeing your age and start measuring your words.

To my peers, let me say that earning the respect and admiration of your elders—those who have lived, loved, and suffered more than we know, the very ones who sometimes shake their heads at our new way of thinking and our modern slang—is way more important than getting likes and applause from people who know nothing about you. The Grand Old Party might be old, but they are not out of touch. They are wise beyond our years. They care deeply about our future, probably more than we do. And we would be right to listen to them more, even if they are not on TikTok.

Clapping Away Our Integrity and Reason

Applause culture makes integrity expensive. This is especially corrosive for young people. Growing up with constant feedback trains you to view identity as something negotiated rather than discovered. You learn early that being liked feels like being safe and that being disliked feels like being in danger. That association is hard to break. It explains why so many people feel anxious even when nothing is objectively wrong. Their sense of worth is tethered to reaction. But that tether is fragile.

The moment applause becomes the measure of truth, reasoning becomes optional. Why reason when you can perform? Why persuade when you can posture? Why listen when listening might cost you points with your own side? This is how echo chambers form. Not because people hate conversation, but because conversation is risky in an environment addicted to affirmation.

As platforms grow and opportunities expand, the temptation grows with them. It is intoxicating to watch numbers climb. It is validating to be quoted, shared, and praised.

There is nothing inherently wrong with recognition. The danger comes when recognition becomes the reason rather than the result. When that happens, speech becomes performative. Conviction becomes conditional. And truth becomes negotiable.

This is where applause culture quietly kills conversation. People stop reasoning together (remember the teaching from Isaiah?) because reasoning does not guarantee affirmation. It requires vulnerability. It risks disagreement. It exposes weak arguments and forces refinement. Applause, by contrast, rewards certainty without scrutiny. It celebrates confidence regardless of content. But confidence detached from truth is just arrogance with better marketing.

The addiction to applause also explains why so many public figures sound the same (that, and the rise in the use of AI to create or sanitize writing). Language converges. Phrases repeat. Talking points harden into scripts. People learn what works and repeat it endlessly, not because it is true, but because it is safe. Original thought becomes rare because originality carries risk. And when originality disappears, so does progress.

A culture addicted to applause cannot sustain conversation because conversation demands something applause culture refuses to give: honesty without guarantees.

A culture addicted to applause cannot sustain conversation because conversation demands something that applause culture refuses to give: honesty without guarantees.

Applause addiction does not just distort what people say. It reshapes how they think. When affirmation becomes the reward structure, people begin to anticipate reactions before they ever articulate beliefs. Arguments are filtered through imagined audiences. Words are chosen not for precision but for impact. The internal question shifts from "Is this true?" to "How will this be received?" That shift happens quietly, but once it takes root, it governs everything.

This is why so much of our public discourse feels hollow. People are not lying outright. They are curating. They are trimming away anything that might complicate the narrative or cost them approval. They speak in absolutes because absolutes travel better. They avoid nuance because nuance requires patience. Over time, the language becomes flatter, sharper, and less human.

This dynamic is not limited to the Left or the Right. It infects everyone who mistakes attention for influence. The outrage economy thrives on this confusion. Algorithms reward emotional spikes because emotion keeps people engaged. Calm reasoning does not. Long-form explanation does not. Admitting uncertainty does not. So, the system quietly trains people to abandon those habits. And the cost is credibility.

The most dangerous part of applause addiction is that it feels like courage. Speaking loudly, attacking opponents, and dominating conversation can look like strength. In reality, it is often insecurity masquerading as conviction. True confidence does not require constant validation. It can withstand silence. It can endure criticism. It can reason without flinching.

This is why cancel culture and applause culture are inseparable. Cancelation is simply the negative side of the same coin. When affirmation is the highest good, rejection becomes the ultimate punishment. The fear of being cast out keeps people in line. It teaches them to monitor their words, align their opinions, and signal loyalty constantly. That fear is what makes silence feel rational, and conformity feel virtuous. But conformity is not unity. It is compliance.

The most powerful censorship tool today isn't the ban; it's the algorithm. Once people learn that truth costs likes, they begin editing themselves long before anyone tells them to stop. Applause is the cheapest drug in politics. It gives instant validation, requires no conviction, and slowly destroys anyone who relies on it to decide what they believe.

I have seen how quickly people will abandon conversation to protect applause. They stop engaging critics. They block dissenters. They retreat into echo chambers where they are guaranteed affirmation. They tell themselves they are preserving their mental health or protecting their platform.

In reality, they are insulating themselves from the very process that sharpens thought and builds resilience.

This is why so many public figures crumble under pressure. They have never learned to withstand disapproval. Their confidence is borrowed, not earned. When the applause fades or turns hostile, they panic. They apologize for truths they once defended. They rewrite history. They distance themselves from positions they held just months earlier. The addiction demands maintenance, and maintenance requires compromise.

Reasoning, by contrast, builds something sturdier. It creates internal coherence. It forces beliefs to align with reality rather than reaction. It prepares people for disagreement because disagreement is expected, not feared. That is why reason is dangerous to systems built on control. A person who can reason does not need constant guidance. They can evaluate claims, resist manipulation, and stand firm under pressure.

Applause addiction undermines all of that.

The most sobering realization is that this addiction often hides behind the language of compassion. People justify silence or performance by claiming they do not want to hurt others. They frame conformity as kindness. But kindness that refuses to reason is not kindness at all. It is avoidance. And avoidance does not heal. It allows lies to fester unchallenged.

The hardest place to confront applause addiction is not in the movements we oppose, but in the ones we claim as our own. It is easy to point at the Left and diagnose its obsession with validation, its fixation on trends, its reliance on emotional theater. It is much harder to admit that the same disease exists on the Right, just dressed in different language and rewarded by different crowds.

> ***Applause addiction does not care about ideology. It cares about attention.***

Applause addiction does not care about ideology. It cares about attention. This is where many well-intentioned people lose their footing. They confuse being bold with being abrasive. They mistake shock value for courage. They equate cruelty with strength because cruelty gets clicks. And when that posture is rewarded, it spreads. People learn that they can bypass the hard work of persuasion by saying something outrageous enough to dominate the moment. But domination is not leadership, and it has no courage.

True courage is not measured by how loudly you speak or how many people cheer. It is measured by how consistently you speak the truth, even when it costs you applause—especially when it costs you applause.

Many of us are enamored by athletes, especially those who have the strength and commitment to battle the elements, such as in the heat of a marathon or in the cold snow of a football game (which I have never experienced, living in Alabama, but they say this really happens). I love college football. I understand why we call the players "gladiators." I also agree with Mark Twain: "It is curious that physical courage should be so common in the world, and moral courage so rare."[10]

The kind of courage I'm talking about is rare in an applause-driven culture because it is cultivated internally rather than externally. It is built through conviction, not validation. It allows a person to withstand criticism without collapsing and to resist flattery without drifting.

This is where my generation has a choice to make. We can continue performing for each other, mistaking reaction for impact and validation for truth. Or we can recover the discipline of reasoning, even when it is uncomfortable, even when it costs us attention, even when it means standing alone for a season.

Breaking the addiction to applause does not mean rejecting affirmation entirely. It means refusing to let affirmation dictate belief. It means being willing to speak when the crowd is silent and to stay silent when the crowd demands noise. It means anchoring identity in something sturdier than likes or followers.

Scripture offers that anchor repeatedly. Our worth comes from Whose we are and what He says about us. Our calling is not contingent on approval. We are accountable to truth, not to trends. When that framework is lost, people drift. When it is restored, courage becomes possible again.

Scripture never treats truth as optional or dangerous. There is wisdom throughout the Bible, especially in the Book of Proverbs, which not only tells you and me about who God is, but also who we are and how we should live. One of my favorite verses as it relates to this topic is Proverbs 23:23: "Buy the truth and do not sell it, wisdom, instruction and insight as well." Awesome! The truth matters more than anything else. But what should we do with it once we have it? That is where all of those "one anothers" of Scripture come in. In Paul's letter to the church in the city of Ephesus, he tells the people: "I urge you to live a life worthy of the calling you have received. Be completely humble and gentle; be patient, bearing with one another in love. Make every effort to keep the unity of the Spirit through the bond of peace."[1] Then, following some explanation about how Jesus is God and how He is the one who defines the reality in which we all live, and after arguing that some people are cunning and crafty and deceitful, he tells the people of the church not to be like them, saying, "Instead, [live] speaking the truth in love . . ."[2]

The Bible treats truth as something to be spoken courageously, in love, which implies both clarity and care. Love without truth is sentimentality. Truth without love is brutality. Conversation is where love and truth must meet. Applause culture tears them apart by rewarding emotion without substance and conviction without accountability. The voices of our culture tell us to love unconditionally (especially ourselves) without ever having to ask questions about what the truth really is or where it comes from.

Conversation depends on the courage to speak the truth, with love, knowing what truth is. You cannot reason with someone if you are constantly checking the crowd. You cannot listen honestly if you are afraid of how listening will be perceived. You cannot persuade if persuasion might cost you applause.

---

1. Ephesians 4:1–3.
2. Ephesians 4:15.

The way forward is not to become quieter or louder, but clearer. We need a culture of clarity that cuts through noise, exposes performance, and invites challenge.

If we want to revive the lost art of conversation, we have to be willing to let applause go. We have to decide that speaking the truth matters more than being liked. We have to recover the humility to reason together and the confidence to stand firm when reasoning leads us to uncomfortable truths.

A culture addicted to applause will resist that invitation. A people committed to truth must accept it anyway. But doing that requires remembering something our politics often forgets: people matter more than platforms.

There was a time in America when fierce political opponents could still share a meal and laugh together. President Ronald Reagan and Democratic Speaker of the House Tip O'Neill battled each other all day on Capitol Hill, then famously shared drinks together in the evening. Supreme Court justices Antonin Scalia and Ruth Bader Ginsburg disagreed on almost every major legal issue of their time, yet remained close friends who vacationed together and attended the opera side by side. Today, relationships like that are often discouraged or even punished. A politician, commentator, or influencer who shows too much respect for someone on the other side risks backlash from their own audience for "platforming the enemy."

The result is predictable: applause replaces persuasion, tribal loyalty replaces truth, and the very conversations that could strengthen the country are abandoned in favor of viral moments.

In today's attention economy, humiliating your opponent earns applause. Talking to them risks criticism from your own side. But if we care more about clicks than conversation, we will eventually wake up in a country where nobody knows how to persuade anyone anymore.

PART II
WHAT IT'S DOING TO US

Chapter 4
Stopping Debate and Creating Division

I love argument. I love debate. I don't expect anyone just to sit there and agree with me, that's not their job.

—Margaret Thatcher

The Left wants you to believe debate is violence and disagreement is hate because if they can redefine words, they can control outcomes. A free society can survive disagreement; it cannot survive fear of disagreement.

One of the most effective lies of the modern age is the idea that disagreement is dangerous. We are told, explicitly and implicitly, that debate fractures communities, argument breeds hatred, and unity requires compliance and silence.

Under the banner of harmony, we are urged to suppress dissent, smooth over differences, and avoid conversations that might make people uncomfortable. The result is not peace. It is paralysis.

Debate is not division. Avoidance is.

Division happens when people stop engaging honestly with one another and begin retreating into camps defined by suspicion and resentment. Debate, by contrast, assumes something profoundly hopeful: that truth exists, people are capable of reasoning, and disagreement does not require dehumanization. A society that cannot debate is not united. It is merely quiet.

People ask all the time how I deal with the hate. At some point in the last few months, the criticism stopped feeling political and started feeling spiritual, not because of ideology, but because of *weight*. I realized this wasn't about winning arguments or losing followers anymore. It was about stewardship. About whether I would use the platform I had been given, however imperfectly, or bury it out of fear.

How could I embrace all of the "one anothers" of Scripture if I ran away? How might I be able to "Offer hospitality to one another without grumbling,"[1] or "Have equal concern for one another"[2] without being in the arena? The Bible tells—no, commands—Christians that we "should use whatever gift he has received to serve others."[3] I'd already told God I wanted to be a light in the darkness of politics;

1. 1 Peter 4:9.
2. 1 Corinthians 12:25.
3. 1 Peter 4:10.

how could I run away from such a stewardship opportunity in the making?

I have to stay; it is my act of love.

Today, God's truth and my love for people stand in stark contrast to what I refer to as the "Compassion Industrial Complex." It's the reason society tells us we can't debate. Hurting somebody's feelings is riskier than civil discourse, so "having compassion for your neighbor" is the excuse given.

During the COVID-19 pandemic, Americans watched the debate itself become suspect. Questioning policy decisions (not rejecting science), but asking about tradeoffs, proportionality, and long-term consequences, was often treated as a moral failure. Such voices of power, including former chief medical advisor to the president Anthony Fauci, and his wicked COVID-19 step-siblings, and nearly every mainstream media host and "opinionist," crushed the questions. Dissenting voices weren't engaged; they were labeled dangerous. This moment trained millions of people to associate curiosity with harm. The long-term damage wasn't just political; it was psychological. A population taught not to ask questions will eventually stop believing it has the right to answers.

Following the assassination of Charlie Kirk, there were a lot of voices talking about free speech and the value of open, honest debate. An op-ed in the *Chicago Star* titled "Disagreement Is Not Dangerous: The Lesson Charlie Kirk Leaves Behind," captured the moment well:

> The issue isn't Kirk. The problem is our culture. College campuses and society in general are teaching young

> people that if you think differently, you're considered dangerous. If you question too much, you're labeled extreme. As Gen Xers, we grew up differently. We spoke our minds, we listened to people who disagreed with us, and then we met in the Taco Bell parking lot to blast music and hang out. Nobody was keeping score.
>
> Today, everything is about choosing sides and weighing every word so nobody's feelings get hurt. That's not debate, and it's not dialogue. That's fear. And it's why I like being a journalist and a writer. I can use my voice to express myself respectfully, and if you don't like it, please feel free to keep scrolling. Respect is earned. Disagreement doesn't have to lead to violence.[1]

I, too, like being a writer. It is how I express love for God, my neighbors, and the truth. That, and I do enjoy the art of debating.

Truth welcomes scrutiny because it survives it. Lies demand insulation. When questioning becomes taboo, it is not because a society is strong; it is because it is fragile and terrified of exposure. Healthy disagreement is the mark of confidence, not chaos. And it is a hallmark of freedom.

Thinking of another letter written by a follower of Jesus, this time a man named Peter, Scripture does not treat freedom as fragile or dangerous; it treats it as a responsibility. In a letter Peter wrote to the church at large, kind of like an open letter, one that would have been copied and passed along to neighboring house churches, Peter's instruction is clear: "Live as people who are free, not using your freedom as a cover-up for evil, but living as servants of God."[1] Now, some people who have a tendency toward anarchy might only show you the first portion of this verse: "Live as people who are free." And Bible-teaching preachers who want you to change your behavior might focus on the last portion: "living as servants of God." But I want you to see the context and focus on the middle of the verse.

This one comes in the middle of a chapter on how to live as people of God. It also comes in the middle of a thought on authority and government.

> Be subject for the Lord's sake to every human institution, whether it be to the emperor as supreme, or to governors as sent by him to punish those who do evil and to praise those who do good. For this is the will of God, that by doing good you should put to silence the ignorance of foolish people. Live as people who are free, not using your freedom as a cover-up for evil, but living as servants of God. Honor everyone. Love the brotherhood. Fear God. Honor the emperor.[2]

The freedom to live as free people is not a license to do whatever you want, whenever you want. It is a gift given to us so we can, within the boundaries of God's will, and in a civil society with governments, institutions, and laws, do good and "put to silence the ignorance of foolish people." That does not give me, you, or any politician, media personality, or

1. 1 Peter 2:16, ESV.
2. 1 Peter 2:13–17, ESV.

scientist the right to silence anyone. This is not a freedom to dominate or deceive. But it is the encouragement we need to know it is okay to challenge people's foolish ideas and ignorance in an honoring and loving way. And this is how every person, Christian or not, can help make America talk again. With humility, we can support the laws of our country, praise the people who do good, call out foolishness and ignorance for what they are, and live as righteous human beings who can do great things by the grace of God.

When Compassion Submits to Control

Economist Milton Friedman warned that "a society that puts equality before freedom will get neither,"[2] and nowhere is that clearer than in speech policing. Unity built on coerced agreement is not unity at all. It is silence with better branding. Free societies argue loudly because they trust the truth. Unfree ones suppress debate because they don't.

The modern allergy to debate is not rooted in compassion. It is rooted in control. When debate is framed as harm, authority no longer needs to justify itself. If disagreement itself is suspect, then power becomes insulated from challenge. This is why the language of "safety" is so often deployed to shut down discussion. Safety, in this context, does not mean protection from violence or coercion. It means protection from having to defend one's beliefs. That protection comes at a steep cost.

> ***The modern allergy to debate is not rooted in compassion. It is rooted in control.***

A culture that avoids debate does not eliminate conflict. It delays it. Suppressed disagreements do not disappear. They ferment. They harden. And when they eventually surface, they do so without the moderating influence of conversation. Debate is how societies release pressure gradually. Silence allows it to build until something breaks.

This dynamic is visible everywhere. People are told not to ask certain questions, not to challenge certain claims, and not to articulate certain beliefs. Bakers are penalized for declining to participate in "wedding" ceremonies that glorify gay men. Mattress sellers have their bank accounts closed for asking questions about the integrity of our election systems and processes. Students get ostracized for quoting the Bible in their essays. And shoppers are removed from stores for not wearing masks. Thus, we are all learning to comply publicly while dissenting privately.

Over time, the gap between what people say and what they think widens. Trust erodes. Institutions lose credibility. And when trust collapses, even legitimate authority is questioned. "Democracy" is now used to shut down debate, not invite it. When democracy is treated as fragile, citizens are treated as dangerous.

The fear of debate often masquerades as moral concern, and a compassionate one, at that. People insist that some ideas are too dangerous to be discussed, that certain perspectives should be excluded for the greater good. Politicians and doctors who ascribe to Marxist ideas, even if they don't know it, tell us we must give children puberty blockers so they don't kill themselves. Liberal preachers (none of whom are really pastors) tell us that we have to support a woman's right to kill her unborn baby, otherwise the woman's life might be harmed by unexpected hardship. And when those of us who dare to challenge the ignorance and foolishness dare raise our hands, ask a question, or boldly object, we are shamed, told to shut up and sit down, or kicked out of the school, church, club, or company that we dare question. Our sincere desire to do good, to have and show compassion, is too often disregarded just so the people who have the control today can keep it. And to call debate "hate" just might be the most successful way to control anyone, anywhere.

Disregarding Debate

Have you noticed that genuine disagreement is declining in mainstream media? A 2025 academic analysis of US cable news programming found that the proportion of genuine disagreement on prime-time shows has dropped by roughly one-third over the past decade, with segments often functioning as echo chambers rather than forums for contesting ideas.[3] It has been a long time since *Hannity & Colmes* went silent on Fox News in 2009, and we seemed to go with them. I can't imagine a show like this anymore, where two hosts—in the spirit of Sean Hannity, a conservative, and Alan Colmes, a liberal—respectfully debate current events through the lens of differing viewpoints. Why is this? I think those who control the media truly want to control the masses. And if they don't want full control of you and me, the heart of America, they want control of our wallets so we can help pad theirs and the bank accounts of their advertisers.

Performative unity on TV looks peaceful on the surface. It might even remind some of us of the beauty of a church choir when all the participants are singing from the same song sheet, and the music moves us. In those moments, we don't want someone to sing off-key. We don't want one person to unexpectedly step in front of the choir and belt out a hip-hop version of "Amazing Grace." We like the uniformity. We like the continuity. We like the performance. But living in a free society does not mean performing in the same choir. But out of "compassion," too many people avoid hard topics. Dissent is labeled disruptive. And institutions celebrate consensus.

But beneath the surface of the appearance of unity, resentment grows. People feel unheard. They disengage. And eventually, they stop trusting the very structures meant to hold them together. Debate is the antidote to that decay. It allows disagreement without dissolution. It makes space for correction without cancelation. It recognizes that unity built on silence is brittle, while unity built on truth is resilient. Debate does not guarantee agreement, but it preserves relationships by treating opponents as conversers rather than enemies.

This is why authoritarian systems always restrict debate. They understand its power. A population capable of reasoning publicly is difficult to manipulate. Debate decentralizes authority by forcing claims to stand on their merits rather than their enforcement.

A free society depends on this dynamic. Without debate, freedom becomes symbolic rather than substantive. People may technically be free to speak, but culturally conditioned not to. That kind of freedom is freedom in name only.

If we want unity, we must stop fearing disagreement. If we want peace, we must stop confusing quiet with health.

And if we want freedom to endure, we must be willing to use it responsibly, even when doing so is uncomfortable.

The future of American politics won't be decided by who has the loudest base, but by who is brave enough to expand the table.

> ***The future of American politics won't be decided by who has the loudest base, but by who is brave enough to expand the table.***

A Bronx Tale

In the final weeks of the 2024 presidential election, when most campaigns were hiding in safe zip codes and friendly media studios, President Trump did something that left political scientists, pundits, and party elites completely baffled: he announced a rally in the Bronx. Not a swing suburb. Not a red-leaning county dressed up as outreach. The Bronx, as deep blue as it gets, a place Republicans are told not to bother with, much less show up. It was the kind of decision every consultant warns against, and every focus group would have vetoed. And yet, there he was, standing in a packed field, surrounded by thousands of people who had been written off as unreachable.[4]

That rally alone answers one of the most important political questions of our time: How did Trump pull off the greatest comeback in modern American history? How did a man who had been arrested in Georgia, written off by the media, counted out by the establishment, and mocked as politically finished end up serving fries at McDonald's and redecorating the Oval Office all in the same year?

The answer wasn't magic. It wasn't luck. It was conversation. Trump refused to accept the lie that certain communities were "off limits." He rejected the idea that politics is about staying inside your bubble and preaching to your choir. Instead, he showed up where he wasn't supposed to be, spoke to people who weren't supposed to listen, and treated Americans not as demographic checkboxes but as citizens worth engaging.

That Bronx rally wasn't an isolated stunt; it was part of a broader strategy that flipped the old rules of politics upside down. I talked to Trump about joining TikTok while the establishment was still debating whether young people even mattered. He sat down for three-hour podcasts instead of just relying on seven-minute cable news hits. He streamed rallies, showed up at college football games, threw hot dogs into student sections, and talked directly to voters without a script. While other politicians tried to carefully manage optics, Trump leaned into authenticity. And whether you loved him or hated him, you couldn't deny one thing: he was talking with people, not at them.

As a result, he did something the GOP had been told for years was impossible. He cracked open three voter blocs that Republicans were never supposed to touch: independents, disenchanted Democrats, and young voters. People who didn't feel seen or heard by the Republican Party suddenly did. Communities that hadn't been asked for their opinions suddenly were. And it worked, not because every voter agreed with him on every issue, but because he showed them enough respect to show up and make his case. That's what conversation does. It humanizes politics. It disrupts assumptions. It forces both sides to reckon with reality instead of caricatures.

The lesson here is bigger than one rally or one election. We have to stop treating Americans as if they are only voters. And we cannot treat voters as the means to one-time wins or election-cycle experiments. If we want to keep the momentum toward renewing the good that is America, if we want to keep winning, we have to keep the door open. We have to keep talking. We have to keep expanding the tent instead of shrinking it out of fear. The Bronx rally was proof of concept: when you show up, speak plainly, and refuse to surrender entire communities to the loudest voices on the Left, you don't just change polling. You change the conversation. And changing the conversation is how you change the country.

Debating Tyranny

Calling disagreement "violence" is the laziest form of tyranny. If words are violence, then, as I alluded to in the opening of this chapter, power belongs to whoever defines vocabulary. But for just a moment, would you indulge me in a bit of levity before we continue? I think words matter, but interestingly, certain words matter in a completely different way than they did years, decades, and even centuries ago. *Reader's Digest* compiled a list of words that mean what you think they do, but they didn't mean that years ago. Here are a few that make me smile or scratch my head:

- In 1300, the meaning of wench was "a young girl or a servant."[5]
- In 1303, the meaning of villain was "a farmhand or peasant."

- In 1400, the meaning of naughty was "having nothing, or poor or needy."
- In 1175, the meaning of awful was "full of awe, or worthy of reverence."
- In 1800, the original meaning of guy was "a grotesquely dressed person."

Wait. So, what you are telling me is that the people who define what words mean decided that a young servant girl was a wench, and a peasant was a villain. And they were naughty if they had nothing and awful if they had reverence. And that anyone who didn't dress like them was just a guy, a regular Joe. Wow! Words really do change, perhaps because of the elites who are trying to change themselves into the upper-class they so long to be, just so they can feel safe in a world they cannot control any more than a football can control where it lands after being thrown.

The modern fixation on "safety" has quietly redefined what debate is allowed to be. Safety, once understood as protection from physical harm or coercion, has been expanded to include protection from discomfort, challenge, and even exposure to ideas that contradict personal beliefs. Under this redefinition, debate itself becomes suspect, not because it is violent, but because it is unsettling. That shift has profound consequences.

When discomfort is treated as harm, disagreement becomes a moral offense. The person who challenges an idea is no longer a participant in dialogue, but a threat to emotional well-being, because, as Mark Twain said, "Few things are harder to put up with than the annoyance of a good example."[6] When a person raises a hand, asks a question, or pushes back on the narrative, they are no longer simply debating ideas and claims; they are questioning the identity of the people who seek to maintain their grip of control. And the peasant is challenging the upper-class.

The irony is that the rhetoric of safety often creates the very division it claims to prevent. When debate is suppressed, people do not stop disagreeing. They stop talking. Conversations move underground, into spaces where they are reinforced without challenge. Extremes grow sharper because they are never tested. Moderation disappears because it requires dialogue to survive. This is how polarization accelerates.

Debate, when done honestly, slows polarization by forcing people to articulate their positions and confront weaknesses. It humanizes opponents by engaging them directly rather than through caricature. It allows disagreements to be processed in the open rather than weaponized in private. Removing debate does not remove conflict. It removes the mechanism that manages it.

That is why debate is essential to moral clarity. Debate is how societies distinguish between truths that can stand and claims that cannot. It is not a threat to morality; it is a test of it.

Debate requires discipline. It demands listening as well as speaking.

Debate requires discipline. It demands listening as well as speaking. It requires separating people from ideas and refusing to equate disagreement with hostility. That discipline is learned, not innate. And like any discipline, it atrophies when unused.

The current generation has been told that debate is dangerous, words wound irreparably, and silence is kindness. The result is a population less capable of reasoning through disagreement and more vulnerable to manipulation. When people are taught to fear ideas, they become dependent on authorities to filter reality for them. And it is not just the "peasants" who fear debate; it is also the elitists who want to maintain their positions of privilege in their ivory towers. Radio talk show host and author Dennis Prager, whom Charlie Kirk often called his mentor, had this to say about those who refuse to debate ideas, specifically calling out the Left in America:

> Just as not one professor at ASU, who condemned ASU for inviting Charlie Kirk and me to give lectures, agreed to debate me. Because they are cowards. Almost every Leftist is a coward. Liberals are mostly cowards, too. They are not vile like Leftists; some of them are very kind and sweet, but they are as cowardly as Leftists. Cowardice is the human norm. Don't feel bad. But don't feel good either.[7]

I like the distinctions Prager makes. He says liberals are not Leftists. I agree that is the difference between "them" and "they," which I mentioned earlier in the book when I expressed concerns about Marxism and the Left. And he also allows for the distinction between being a coward and acting cowardly. That is so helpful.

While it is true that professors who are unwilling to debate students in class are cowards, because they have the positional authority and right to do so, students who do not raise their hands in class to ask follow-up questions are not necessarily cowards, but they are acting cowardly (which really means they are intent on self-preservation). So, to my classmate who chooses to stay silent, I say, as Prager did, "don't feel bad." And to the professor who chooses to kick a student out of class instead of discussing the question further, "don't feel good about it."

You see, debate preserves agency. It affirms dignity. When people debate, they acknowledge each other's agency. They concede, implicitly, that the person across from them is capable of reason, capable of being persuaded, and worthy of being heard. That acknowledgment is profoundly humanizing. It treats citizens as participants rather than subjects. Removing debate removes that agency, leaving people either disengaged or radicalized. This is why the recovery of debate is not optional. Without it, freedom becomes hollow, and unity becomes performative.

When authoritarian cultures replace debate with simple slogans, they complicate debate. Just look at all the paid protesters interviewed on the streets of Minneapolis, New York City, and Los Angeles in 2026. Video after video shows people chanting and holding up signs with slogans, often with very little ability to communicate why they believe the slogan. They can't give an explanation for why they believe Donald Trump is a racist. They can't give you the names of the ten people they know who will not be able to vote in a secure election because they don't have a valid ID. They can't define what a woman is without using the words "woman" or "feel." Slogans demand repetition and demean humanity. Debate demands understanding and elevates people. A culture saturated with slogans but starved of debate is easy to mobilize and difficult to govern wisely. It reacts quickly but thinks slowly, if at all. Freedom cannot survive in that environment.

In *Mere Christianity*, C. S. Lewis explains that "Christianity is the total plan for the human machine."[8] By machine, he is referring to how human beings live and work and play together as a community. In his chapter on social morality, he references the popular Bible verse, "So in everything, do to others what you have them do to you . . ."[1] and Lewis says, "I cannot learn to love my neighbour [sic] as myself till I learn to love God: and I cannot learn to love God except by learning to obey Him."[9] But, of course, the challenge is that the natural inclination of humanity is to not obey God. Heck, not only do we not obey God, but many of us choose not to even debate God. We simply ignore him because, as Lewis says, "We have all departed from that total plan in different ways, and each of us wants to make out that his own modifications of the original plan is the plan itself."[10] We remove God from the center and put ourselves there instead, because we are reaching for the control we lack. "You will be tempted to provide for yourself, to protect yourself, and to exalt yourself. And at the core of these three is a common impulse, to cast off the fatherhood of God."[11] We would be

1. Matthew 7:12.

wise to contemplate, as Tyler Staton wrote, "There are such far-reaching consequences to this impulse to put the self at center."[12]

Relativism and "your truth" and "my truth" are evidence that we have "cast off the fatherhood of God" and created our own plan, with yours truly at the center. The Left calls debate "hate" because they don't want us modifying their plan. Dare I say we avoid debate because we don't trust in the strength of our plan, but we don't want anyone to modify it? This is why we are being enslaved to ignorance and foolishness instead of doing good and honoring others and God. And one of the ways out of this is through healthy debate that leads to new discoveries of freedom and meaning. Debate keeps freedom alive by exercising it. It gives meaning to people. It normalizes disagreement. It lowers the emotional stakes of conflict. When debate is routine, disagreement does not feel apocalyptic. It becomes part of civic life rather than a threat to it.

Like you, I sometimes doubt we can engage in healthy debate in our polarized culture. But know that hostility dissipates when people are given permission to argue honestly. Not scream. Not posture. Listen. Argue. Explain. Challenge. Defend. Even when agreement is not reached, something valuable happens. Misunderstandings are corrected. Assumptions are exposed. And the temperature drops because the rules are clear.

For Christians living as servants of God, this adds another layer of responsibility. Debate is not about winning at all costs. It is about stewarding truth faithfully. That means resisting the temptation to dominate or humiliate. It means speaking clearly without cruelty and listening seriously without surrender. It means using freedom not as a weapon, but as a tool for understanding. Reflecting on the previous chapter on platforms and the media that control them, I want to leave you with some habits you can begin implementing so you can become more comfortable (or a little less awkward) listening to others as they share ideas that are new to you. Healthy debate requires a posture of listening and learning. If you are going into the conversation to prove your point or "own" the person you are talking to, go for a long walk and remember your grandparents' guidance: "If you don't have anything nice to say, don't say anything at all."

If you are going to repeatedly blame the other person, their associations, or their "derangement syndrome," take a few minutes and Google "all the one anothers in the Bible" and read them before you start the conversation.

If you want to believe you know the truth because you listen to NPR or watch Fox News, and you are just going to repeat talking points from yesterday's show, go read some writings from Paul Krugman, Arianna Huffington, Milton Friedman, or Richard Nixon. Watch some videos on PragerU. Listen to some conservative talk radio. Watch a couple of Sunday morning news shows. Broaden your perspective. Or, better yet, show up to the conversation and do nothing but ask questions. Sincere, curious questions.

Leave the creating of division to the globalists, Marxists, and media elites. As servants of the living God, honor everyone. Love the brotherhood. Fear God. Honor the emperor.

Chapter 5
Cancel Culture and the Fear Economy

Give me liberty or give me death![1]

—Patrick Henry

Nobody wakes up one morning brave. Courage is built the same way movements are built—by small decisions stacked on top of each other until something shifts. Every movement that looks inevitable in hindsight began as something fragile. Before it had momentum, before it had language, before it had leaders and logos, it had people willing to take small risks without any guarantee they would matter. No great shift in history started with certainty. It started with conviction paired with action, usually in moments so ordinary they almost felt insignificant at the time.

It was 1776, and the people of the American colonies were growing more and more concerned with their devolving relationship with England. Author Thomas Paine, observing the world around him, wrote in a pamphlet that would become "The American Crisis," "These are the times that try men's souls."[2]

These very words can be said in 2026, in the aftermath of our government's terrible response to the COVID-19 pandemic, the rise of transgender ideology, the intolerance of Black Lives Matter (BLM) activists, and the concerted effort by the Left in America to gain more and more control by abusing illegal immigrants, exchanging hope and dollars for their votes.

Each of us has a responsibility to do our part to preserve freedom, not just for ourselves and our neighbors, but for our children and the future of America. We need to have the courage to ignore the comforting lie that movements are born from massive moments. From speeches that shake the ground. From viral videos. From sweeping elections or dramatic confrontations. Those moments matter, but they are never the beginning. They are the visible crest of a wave that formed quietly, one decision at a time, long before anyone was paying attention. And the beginning was always with a small risk by someone like you and me. Small risks are where truth begins to be embodied, spoken, defended, and lived.

For us, that embodiment almost always begins with a risk that feels minor but costs something real. A raised hand. A hard question. A decision not to repeat a lie. A willingness to be misunderstood. A choice to speak when silence would be easier. These moments do not feel like history being made. They feel awkward. They feel risky. They feel lonely. And that is precisely why most people avoid them. Movements do not need everyone. They need enough people willing to take the first step, willing to be booed, willing to be canceled.

One of the easiest ways to pressure people into silence today is to accuse them of being "too political" the moment they speak with conviction, but that tactic only works if we accept it. As Eric Metaxas warns in *Letter to the American Church*, "So if someone attacks us for being political, we must cheerfully ignore their criticism. To allow the voices of this world to silence us in this way is precisely how the German Church was silenced." That warning forces a deeper, more personal question, because silence usually starts long before public pressure. It starts when our lives don't match what we claim to believe. Metaxas puts it bluntly: "Does how I live show God that I actually believe what I claim to believe? Or does how I live show God that actually I do not believe what I claim to believe?"[3] A culture doesn't lose its moral voice overnight; it loses it when people slowly decide it's easier to stay quiet than to live and speak like their convictions are real.

Most of us believe something is broken in America. And many of us believe part of the cause is that there is something deeply broken in American higher education where a certain subset of students (think Christians and conservatives) feel they must hide their beliefs, or worse, pretend to be liberals, just to survive a class. There is something calculated and calloused going on in our universities, and the November

2025 case out of the University of Oklahoma is impossible to ignore.

A psychology student named Samantha Fulnecky failed an opinion-based assignment because she quoted the Bible in her essay on gender roles. The professor, a self-identified transgender instructor, marked her down not because her work lacked structure or clarity, but because her reasoning came from a worldview the professor didn't personally accept. And this is exactly the kind of thing students pulled me aside to tell me about at every single school I visited—stories whispered quietly, like they were confessing something dangerous, because that's how it feels to them.

Let's be very clear: If your grade depends on agreeing with your professor, the class isn't teaching; it's indoctrinating. But this incident isn't just about one professor or one school. It's a symptom of a culture that has quietly taken root in academia over the last decade: a culture that demands uniformity, punishes dissent, and treats Christian or conservative students as unwelcome intruders in their own classroom. And nobody should have to pay thousands of dollars in tuition just to be told their beliefs are unacceptable.

The Left loves to use phrases like "diversity" and "inclusion," but those words somehow never apply to diversity of thought or inclusion of faith. You can quote Sigmund Freud, Michel Foucault, or the latest TikTok influencer in your paper, but bring in Scripture, and suddenly you've committed an academic sin. Students told me they've had professors praise "open dialogue" on the first day of class, only to spend the rest of the semester making it clear which opinions will cost them their grade. The irony is almost too rich to ignore: universities that preach tolerance have somehow become the least tolerant places in American life.

The purpose of education used to be equipping students to think critically, debate honestly, and evaluate competing ideas. Today, too many classrooms function like echo chambers where disagreement is treated as a threat, not an opportunity for honest conversation.

And for Christian and conservative students, the message is loud and clear: conform or be punished. And again, I watched this play out in real time. At one campus, a student waited until everyone else had left just to whisper to me, "What do I say when my professor mocks Christianity?" At another, a student told me their professor openly admits to grading conservatives more harshly because of our "dangerous worldview." These aren't "internet stories." These are real kids, with real fears, looking for permission to breathe.

Let's stop pretending this is coming from "educators." These are activists wearing professor badges, as many universities have abandoned the idea that a classroom is a marketplace of ideas. Instead, they define it as a training ground for ideological alignment. Students aren't encouraged to ask questions; they're expected to memorize the "correct" answers. And if those answers conflict with their faith, their upbringing, their moral framework, or even basic common sense? Too bad. Students told me they've learned to read the room before they speak, to scan for who's listening, to choose their words cautiously—not because they lack conviction, but because they know the wrong sentence can follow them for four years.

But here's the most important part: students see it. They feel it. And they're tired of it.

Young people today are more aware of double standards than ever. They can see when criticism is selective, when biases are obvious, and when the person grading their paper cares more about politics than teaching. And when a student gets failed for citing the Bible in an opinion essay, the bias isn't subtle. It's a billboard. The result? Silence, fear, and self-censorship. And that's exactly what many professors want.

If students are intimidated into silence, the activist-educator never has to defend their ideas. They never have to justify their assumptions. They never have to engage in a real debate.

The easiest classroom to control is the one where the conservative students have already learned to keep their heads down. But that silence comes at a cost, not only for students, but for the integrity of academia itself. When only one viewpoint is allowed, education becomes propaganda. When students stop asking hard questions, learning stops entirely. And when professors punish religious or political identity, they aren't just breaking trust. They're breaking the very purpose of their profession. And that cost is exactly why students kept lining up after my events—not for selfies but for reassurance. Reassurance that they're not crazy, not alone, and not wrong for refusing to surrender their beliefs.

The solution isn't complicated. It doesn't require federal investigations or massive new bureaucracies. It just requires courage.

Sunlight fixes this. Exposure fixes this.

The truth will set you free.

Every time a story like the OU case goes public, it forces universities to confront what they've allowed to fester.

Administrators don't change because they suddenly rediscover their moral compass. They change because parents start asking questions, donors start demanding accountability, and lawmakers start paying attention. Not unlike what happened in the middle of the COVID-19 pandemic, when parents heard what was going on "in the classroom" because their kids were forced to be at home, trying to learn online.

The more students tell their stories, the harder it becomes for universities to hide behind empty slogans about inclusion. And nothing reveals hypocrisy faster than a Christian student getting failed for having a belief rooted in Scripture.

Students shouldn't have to pretend to be liberals just to pass a class. They shouldn't feel pressured to rewrite their faith to avoid offending a professor. They shouldn't have to choose between truth and a GPA. And they certainly shouldn't be punished for believing something that billions of people across the globe believe, and have believed for thousands of years.

It's time for students, especially conservative and Christian students, to stand firm. Not with anger, not with outrage, but with clarity, confidence, and conviction. Because the moment you force a student to deny their beliefs in exchange for a passing grade, you haven't educated them. You've coerced them. And coercion has no place in a classroom.

If universities truly care about academic excellence, genuine diversity, and preparing young people for the world they're about to lead, then it's time for them to practice the tolerance they preach. Until then, sunlight will continue to expose what's happening behind closed doors, and students must continue refusing to roll over.

Sadly, while I'm talking about my experiences (and the experiences of tens of thousands of students like me), this is not limited to higher education. Cancel culture has its grip on everyone, everywhere, and this isn't some modern discovery.

Even the Stoic philosopher Epictetus saw it centuries ago. He warned in *The Enchiridion of Epictetus* that if you really want to live by conviction, you should expect to be mocked, writing,

> If you have an earnest desire of attaining to philosophy, prepare yourself from the very first to be laughed at . . . if you adhere to the same point, those very persons who at first ridiculed will afterwards admire you.

That's exactly how it works now. The moment you stop drifting with the crowd and start standing for something—faith, truth, moral clarity, love of country—the reaction is almost predictable: eye-rolling first, respect later.

The temptation is to soften your stance just enough to avoid the ridicule, but Epictetus understood what we keep relearning the hard way: if you cave to the pressure, you don't gain acceptance. You just lose credibility.

Real leadership, in any generation, starts with the willingness to stand firm long enough, through the fear, waiting for the laughter to fade.

Overcoming Recent History by Remembering Our Founding History

When I stepped into the role to chair the Republican National Committee's inaugural Youth Advisory Council in January of 2023,[4] I was met with a blunt reality the party had been avoiding for decades: Republicans had not won the youth vote in the modern era. Not since Bill Clinton pulled out a saxophone on MTV's "Rock the Vote" stage in 1992[5] had the GOP figured out how to speak to young Americans in a way that felt human, relevant, and real. For thirty years, Democrats owned the cultural megaphone, and Republicans kept acting surprised by the results.

But more importantly, and what I really want you to understand, is that when party leaders asked me for advice, I was scared. I could have easily canceled myself before I got the courage to speak my mind. I could have let the voices telling me that I was too young, too Boomer, too naïve, boo me off stage and out of the conference room. I could have run away from the debate before it even started. Cancel culture has a way of silencing us, even if we are the ones quieting our own voices.

So, when party leaders asked me for advice, I mustered the courage to tell them what I thought, knowing that it had likely been discussed before: the days of running an ad in the Sunday paper and calling it youth outreach were over.

My generation does not wait for permission to engage. We don't consume politics the way our parents did. We scroll, we stream, we listen, we watch, and we decide. And if you're not showing up where we are, you're not showing up at all.

With the agreement of the RNC, I helped push the party to launch its first-ever Creator Program,[6] credentialing independent voices and influencers who speak directly to millions of young Americans without the filter of legacy media and giving them a front row seat to Trump's rallies, the convention, and debates. I encouraged candidates to step out of the safe, scripted television bubble and into long-form podcast conversations where authenticity can't be faked, and conviction can't be hidden. And yes, I talked face-to-face with President Trump, five separate times, and made the case that modern platforms, including social media apps the political class loves to sneer at, were not optional anymore. They were essential.

The results spoke louder than any focus group ever could. According to exit polling conducted by CNN and ABC News, President Trump walked away with a stunning 44 percent of Gen Z voters under the age of thirty, an outcome Republicans were told for years was mathematically impossible.[7] He also held 46 percent of voters between the ages of thirty and forty-four, a demographic dominated by millennials.[8] That kind of performance doesn't happen by accident. It happens when a campaign chooses connection over caution and conversation over condescension.

And here's the part too many people miss: Now that President Trump is the forty-seventh president, the work doesn't stop. In fact, it matters more than ever. If the campaign phase proved that young Americans are willing to listen, the governing phase must prove they were right to do so.

> ***You don't earn generational trust and then retreat back into old habits.***

You don't earn generational trust and then retreat back into old habits. That's why I believe the next chapter of leadership demands something bolder. Imagine a monthly White House podcast, thirty minutes, once a month, where the president speaks directly to the American people without the distortions of hostile media framing. Not a formal address behind the Resolute Desk. A modern-day fireside chat, streamed globally, rooted in substance instead of soundbites. Imagine a briefing room that doesn't just belong to the same handful of legacy reporters but welcomes creators, podcasters, and independent journalists who actually command the attention of the next generation. Imagine a White House that continues to meet young Americans where they are, including platforms critics dismissed until they started working.

We saw what happens when leaders are willing to adapt. Trump's TikTok account became the fastest-growing account in the platform's history within a week, not because of gimmicks, but because people recognized something rare: authenticity in a political world addicted to performance.

The lesson is simple. Winning so much of Gen Z wasn't a fluke. It wasn't a trend. And it wasn't an accident. It was the product of courage, the courage to talk instead of lecture, to listen instead of assume, and to evolve instead of retreat. If Republicans want to keep this generation, they must keep doing the one thing politics forgot how to do for far too long: Show up, speak plainly, and treat young Americans like adults capable of serious thought.

But here is the problem. I wonder how many of our current elected officials have the courage to discern the truth and fight for it.

When our Founding Fathers signed the Declaration of Independence 250 years ago, they didn't do it for clout. They did it knowing they were signing their own death warrants.

They risked everything—land, family, future—because they believed in something bigger than themselves: the idea that liberty is worth dying for.

Today, we honor that courage with TikTok dances, viral trends, and backyard cookouts. Don't get me wrong, I love fireworks and a good hot dog as much as the next guy. But let's not forget that July 4 isn't just a party. It's a reminder. A warning.

And for my generation, a wake-up call. Because here's the hard truth: We've inherited more freedom than any generation in history, and we're wasting it. We scroll past headlines about the First Amendment being shredded, biological reality being redefined, and unborn children being discarded like trash, and we shrug. We treat patriotism like a costume we wear on the Fourth and toss back in the closet on the Fifth. We've got college kids burning the flag while enjoying the very freedoms it represents. Some even call the American Revolution "colonial oppression," as if they'd prefer to be ruled by a king who didn't even have WiFi.

It's embarrassing. And it's dangerous.

We're told America is the problem. That it's broken. That it's irredeemable. But here's what your professors won't tell you: The American experiment, flawed and imperfect, is still the greatest leap forward for human freedom in world history. The problem isn't America. The problem is, generation after generation, we have not known how to defend it, and we've been told to stop talking about America as if it is something worth talking about.

Freedom isn't just an abstract idea. It's the ability to speak your mind without fear, to worship your God without compromise, to raise your family how you see fit, and to choose your leaders without asking a king. In America, power comes from the people. That's still revolutionary. But it only works if we show up.

For those of us who know the truth, that America is worth saving, we have to be willing stare into the face of cancel culture and still show up. We have to be willing to be booed. We have to grasp that every school board meeting, city council vote, and legislative session is a battlefield for our values, and each forum is an opportunity for debate, even if only to show the world which party refuses to debate.

The Founders gave us a nation. The question now is whether we're strong enough, brave enough, and bold enough to keep it.

The Courage to Be Canceled, Even Just a Little Bit

Movements don't begin with massive courage. They begin when someone decides to stop lying to themselves. Every cultural earthquake starts with a few people taking risks small enough to seem insignificant, until they stack.

When I think of my friend Charlie Kirk, I think of a man who never stopped talking, not in the sense of noise or chatter, but in the sense of conviction. He believed words mattered, that truth spoken boldly could cut through the lies of a culture determined to silence us. Charlie taught me, and so many others in my generation, that when the world tells you to sit down and shut up, that's the exact moment you stand taller and speak louder.

The worst thing we could do right now is go quiet, just to avoid being canceled or booed, and escape the butterflies from the moment you are about to be awkward. That's what the Left and the cultural Marxists want. In their effort to remake God and America into their own image, they hope grief will muzzle us, that fear will keep us silent, and that apathy will win. But silence isn't an option. When good people stop talking, bad ideas take root. When the truth retreats, lies advance. That's why Charlie never stopped showing up, never stopped encouraging, mentoring, and fighting for young voices to be heard.

Charlie believed in us, in Gen Z. He believed our words, our ideas, and our courage could shift the direction of this country. He told me once that when others wrote off my generation as apathetic or distracted, he saw potential. He saw leaders. He saw voices that could not and should not be silenced. That belief became his mission. And because of it, countless young people, myself included, were inspired to pick up the microphone, write the column, or start the conversation others were too afraid to begin.

This is the task before us now: to carry Charlie's mission forward. To make sure his belief in us was not misplaced. To prove that even in moments of loss and uncertainty, our generation will not sit on the sidelines. If we want to honor Charlie, we don't do it with moments of silence. We do it with a movement of voices.

We've all seen how one voice becomes two. Two become a handful. A handful becomes a conversation. And a conversation becomes the largest televised memorial service in human history. Following Charlie's assassination, there were vigils, speeches, conversations, and a whole "I am Charlie Kirk" trend online. The anti-God, anti-America, anti-MAGA movement got a rude awakening and realized that those of us who acknowledge the good leadership of President Trump do so because we love America, not him. And no matter how hard they tried to bring lawfare against President Trump, he is not the only person in their way. Millions and millions of Americans who voted for Donald Trump also identify with Charlie Kirk, Vice President JD Vance, and a host of other patriotic Americans who have the courage to stand and fight. And what are we fighting for? We are fighting for a truth that sets us free, whether that is the singular Truth of biblical Christianity or the broader truth of America being a "shining city on a hill."

That's why I keep thinking about something Ronald Reagan said, that "freedom is never more than one generation away from extinction."[9] He wasn't talking about some far-off threat. He was warning about exactly this moment, when one election could set in motion a change that future generations might never undo.

Canceled by Socialists

When John Winthrop arrived on the shores of America, he called it "a city on a hill," a beacon of hope for the world and a model for Christian charity for all. When I'm flying back to class from speeches late at night, I like to look out the window, seeing all that America is and has to offer, and think about that phrase.

The American Experiment is alive, but it may not be well. There is a creep happening in America, one that seeks to undermine democracy and tear down our shining city. Zohran Mamdani, a self-described Democratic Socialist, relied on young, ignorant, foolish voters to deliver him the mayor's office in New York City. As part of the Left, he sold socialism to my peers: he dressed it up as "compassion," branded capitalism as "greed," and used TikTok to pump millions of young Americans full of "government is your savior" soundbites.

But here's the truth: You don't wake up in a socialist America overnight. It happens slowly, vote by vote, race by race, until one day, the people chanting "liberation" realize they've built their own cage. And once socialism takes hold, it doesn't hand back power.

Just the other day in Auburn, I sat down for lunch with a pastor friend I met after moving here for college. His refusal to be controlled is central to his testimony.

He grew up in Communist Cuba, and what he told me made it clear that socialism is bigger than a TikTok trend. He said kids in his school would sometimes come to class crying on their seventh birthday, because that was the age when the socialist system stopped giving them their daily free milk—and suddenly, the promises of the state didn't feel so generous anymore. He also told me about Christian friends who were punished simply for saying Jesus, not the government, was Lord—believers who were harassed, stripped, beaten, even electrocuted for refusing to treat the state like their god. Sitting there in a quiet Auburn restaurant, it hit me how easy it is for Americans to treat freedom like a theory instead of a miracle. For him, faith and liberty weren't abstract talking points; they were things people suffered for. And it's hard to hear stories like that and not realize how dangerous it is when any government starts demanding the kind of loyalty that belongs to God alone. It was also a reminder that yes, it's scary to be bold and use this platform God has provided for me, but it's nothing compared to the daily persecution Christians in our own hemisphere face, so I think I can handle a few stares or eye rolls for speaking out here as opposed to electrocution there.

I understand that socialism looks trendy to many, but it's not some experiment in a lab. People build rafts out of garbage to flee socialist countries for the chance to live in freedom here. Find me one person who escaped a socialist country, came to America for a new life, and isn't disturbed by the modern-day Left embracing Mamdani's platform. You won't.

This didn't start with Mamdani's campaign. It started in classrooms where gratitude for America was replaced with guilt. In entertainment that mocked faith, family, and free markets. On social media platforms, where dissent is shadow-banned and socialist talking points trend on cue.

Here's what you won't hear on CNN or MSNBC: my generation isn't lost. More and more of us are waking up to the truth that socialism doesn't "level the playing field," it levels the entire country into shared misery. We've seen the countries our professors praise, and we've seen the people who risk everything to escape them. We know the most rebellious thing you can be in 2025 is unapologetically pro-America, pro-faith, and pro-freedom.

For people like my parents and grandparents who turn on their TV screens and see stories like this and wonder how we got here, I understand your concern. But the fight isn't over. There's a growing number of young conservatives who aren't interested in watching the American experiment get dismantled. We intend to keep the promise of this country alive.

Yet, if socialism can win in New York, that beacon of light risks becoming a cautionary tale, a dimmed light signaling to the world that freedom in America was just a temporary experiment. And the truth is, we're not just one generation away from losing it. In New York, the city of 9/11, we lost it. Now, it is time for all of us to get it back.

September 12 and Hope for Tomorrow

In the aftermath of the horrid attack on America on September 11, 2001, we were all Americans. If you were alive, you lived it. If not, you have heard about it. This country, and its Judeo-Christian ethic, was on display for the world to see.

Whether they knew it or not, by God's grace, men and women, boys and girls, old and young, embraced what the Bible calls the "Fruit of the Spirit," which is who Christians become more and more each day, because of the love of God. We become people of "love, joy, peace, patience, kindness, goodness, faithfulness, gentleness, [and] self-control."[1] On this day, almost twenty-five years ago, with the pain and horror in our minds, and love of our neighbors in our hearts, Americans stood unified against the evil that attacked us. It was a moment of unity, one that is lost today, but not forgotten.

In recent decades, high schools around America have started sharing a speech from Ronald Reagan as an example of unity and hope and as a model for civility and discourse.

1. Galatians 5:22–23.

Following the tragic deaths of the "Challenger Seven" astronauts, President Reagan addressed the country:

> Ladies and gentlemen, I'd planned to speak to you tonight to report on the state of the Union, but the events of earlier today have led me to change those plans. Today is a day for mourning and remembering. Nancy and I are pained to the core by the tragedy of the shuttle Challenger. We know we share this pain with all of the people of our country. This is truly a national loss.
>
> Nineteen years ago, almost to the day, we lost three astronauts in a terrible accident on the ground. But we've never lost an astronaut in flight; we've never had a tragedy like this. And perhaps we've forgotten the courage it took for the crew of the shuttle. But they, the Challenger Seven, were aware of the dangers, but overcame them and did their jobs brilliantly. We mourn seven heroes: Michael Smith, Dick Scobee, Judith Resnik, Ronald McNair, Ellison Onizuka, Gregory Jarvis, and Christa McAuliffe. We mourn their loss as a nation together.
>
> For the families of the seven, we cannot bear, as you do, the full impact of this tragedy. But we feel the loss, and we're thinking about you so very much. Your loved ones were daring and brave, and they had that special grace, that special spirit that says, "Give me a challenge, and I'll meet it with joy." They had a hunger to explore the universe and discover its truths. They wished to serve, and they did. They served all of

> us. We've grown used to wonders in this century. It's hard to dazzle us. But for 25 years the United States space program has been doing just that. We've grown used to the idea of space, and perhaps we forget that we've only just begun. We're still pioneers. They, the members of the Challenger crew, were pioneers.
>
> And I want to say something to the schoolchildren of America who were watching the live coverage of the shuttle's takeoff. I know it is hard to understand, but sometimes painful things like this happen. It's all part of the process of exploration and discovery. It's all part of taking a chance and expanding man's horizons. The future doesn't belong to the fainthearted; it belongs to the brave. The Challenger crew was pulling us into the future, and we'll continue to follow them.[10]

For a moment, in the middle of our shock, we were all Americans. President Reagan praised the bravery and courage of those who dared to tame the idea of space. He admired their spirit that says, "Give me a challenge, and I'll meet it with joy." He spoke gently to the schoolchildren, acknowledging their pain and how difficult it is to understand terrible moments when they happen. And he challenged us all, with hope, into the future: "The future doesn't belong to the fainthearted; it belongs to the brave."

My fellow Americans, it is time to be brave. It is time to, as Samantha Fulnecky did, put our faith into action. It is time to walk toward the debate and not from it, just as Charlie did. And it is time to live with hope, just as Ronald Reagan did, because the future is still ours, no matter how many people try to instill fear in our hearts and minds and cancel us along the way.

And to the Gen-Xers and Boomers reading this, do not be afraid. Do not let your hearts be troubled. Know that Charlie put a great deal of confidence in Gen Z. He modeled Jesus to us in a way that matters, and he told us to step up, and we are. Despite headlines about youth disengagement, data suggests that young people remain politically aware and active, just not in predictable ways. According to a national survey of civic knowledge, Gen Z's understanding of political systems is higher than that of Millennials, contradicting stereotypes of ignorance or apathy among young voters.[11] At the same time, political apathy studies show that nearly 20 percent of American youth report not feeling informed enough to vote, highlighting a gap between knowledge and confidence.[12] Meanwhile, social media engagement remains high among youth, with around 96 percent of teenagers using the internet daily and nearly half online almost constantly,[13] meaning digital spaces have become primary arenas for political socialization, for better and worse, influencing how movements grow and how risks are perceived.

While freedom might be "never more than one generation away from extinction," it is always closer than fear wants you to believe. Fear thrives on exaggeration and delay. It tells you that the cost is too high and the timing is wrong. It tells you that you are alone and resistance is futile. But as our conversations continue, as we talk and debate, more and more of us know that fear is a lie, because the truth is setting us free.

Chapter 6
The Loneliest Generation with the Loudest Voices

If silence seems to give approval, then remaining silent is cowardly.[1]

—Eleanor Roosevelt

Conversation used to be the engine of American life. It happened around dinner tables, in churches, in town halls, and on front porches. It was imperfect, often heated, sometimes uncomfortable, but it was understood to be necessary. Disagreement was not seen as a threat to unity but as a test of it. The assumption was that truth could withstand scrutiny and that people, even when wrong, were still worth engaging.

We keep pretending words and mobs don't have consequences, but the numbers tell a darker story. Suicide is now one of the leading causes of death for young Americans, and the crisis isn't abstract; it's exploding in the very generation raised online. Among US high school students, one in five say they've seriously considered suicide, and about one in ten report attempting it.[2] In fact, suicide has become the second-leading cause of death for Americans ages ten to thirty-four, and youth suicide rates rose over 60 percent from 2007 to 2021.[3] That's not just a mental-health statistic; it's a cultural warning light. We've built a digital arena where public shaming spreads instantly, reputations can be destroyed overnight, and mobs celebrate someone's downfall like it's entertainment. Call it cancel culture, call it online outrage, call it whatever makes us feel better—but when humiliation becomes a spectator sport and mercy disappears from public life, fragile people don't just log off. Some break. A society that cheers destruction, even social destruction, shouldn't be shocked when despair follows. Compassion isn't weakness; it's a survival requirement for a country that claims to value human life.

It wasn't always like this, you know. More than two decades ago, Coca-Cola created a brilliant commercial featuring Democrat pundit James Carville and former Republican senator and majority leader Bill Frist. In the commercial, the two are engaged in a political debate during an on-air television show, talking over one another, saying things like, "Democrats have been spreading this far Left agenda . . ."

and "The Republicans are up to their old tricks," and then they both say, at the same time, "They're just plain wrong!" And in this moment, a jinx is called out, and the remedy is for Carville to buy Frist a Coke. They immediately leave the set, grab cold, glass bottles of Coke, and proceed to have a day-long bromance, touring the city on a double-decker bus, visiting a museum, riding Segways, getting their caricatures painted in the park, and taking in a basketball game. The commercial ends with the two clinking their Coke bottles on the stairs of the Capitol building, looking across the mall to the Washington Monument, all while the background music is singing about "A friend like you."[4]

But now, the assumption that truth can withstand security and that people are worth engaging is nearly gone. In its place is a culture that treats conversation as dangerous and silence as responsible. And this silence is leading to lonely people and screaming generations.

People no longer enter conversations to understand or to be understood. Today, too many people enter conversations to win, to score points, or to survive without being noticed. And when that happens, conversation stops serving its purpose and becomes just another weapon.

There's a quiet loneliness that comes with being the person everyone associates with politics. You become the topic people tiptoe around. The one friends in class or at the dining hall hesitate to invite into certain conversations. The one who feels the room shift when something news-related comes up. No one says it out loud, but you feel it, the unspoken request to not make things uncomfortable.

What most people don't realize is that discomfort isn't what drives people like me; it's avoidance. I don't speak because I enjoy tension. I speak because pretending not to care costs more than disagreement ever will. And what am I speaking out about?

> ***The American education system taught an entire generation how to clap, boo, and block, but never how to reason.***

In the last century, the American education system taught an entire generation how to clap, boo, and block, but never how to reason. This culture doesn't produce radicals; it produces silencers, educators, human resources employees, liberal pastors, scientists, and politicians who believe they know best and train others to remain silent for their own good. Students learn quickly that the safest strategy is invisibility. They speak in code. They nod along. They submit papers they don't believe. Not because they lack conviction, but because the institutional cost of honesty is too high. What emerges is not consensus, but quiet resentment and intellectual dishonesty masquerading as harmony.

The result is a generation trained to survive institutions, not challenge them. Universities still market themselves as champions of free inquiry, but in practice, they reward compliance over curiosity. When disagreement becomes a liability, education stops being about truth and starts being about navigation.

There is something profoundly wrong with a system that claims to educate but demands obedience instead of cultivating thoughts. In theory, universities exist to expose students to competing ideas and teach them how to reason. In practice, too many classrooms have become ideological sorting mechanisms where students learn not how to think, but how to comply.

When a student is punished not for poor reasoning but for reasoning from a worldview a professor dislikes, the classroom ceases to be a place of learning and becomes a place of coercion. Grades turn into leverage. Authority turns into intimidation. And the lesson students absorb is simple: Truth is acceptable only when it aligns with power.

Universities love to advertise diversity. But too often, diversity of thought is the only form they refuse to tolerate. Scripture, faith, and traditional moral frameworks are treated as intellectual contraband, allowed nowhere except in ridicule. And the result is not enlightenment, but silence. Silence that benefits the professor. Silence that protects the institution. Silence that costs the student their voice.

False Promises to the Lonely

A generation trained to stay quiet in classrooms will not suddenly become courageous in public life. Worse, we will become more and more isolated and lonely.

I don't believe this is a political problem, as it affects people from every generation across many social and racial backgrounds. I do think it is a moral issue, one that is directly related to the silencing of people with the goal of control. I believe it is the result of Marxist indoctrination that pits old against young, rich against poor, men against women, black against white, brown against black, legal immigrant against illegal alien, and the list goes on and on. And what has this indoctrination led to? Black Lives Matter riots. Mask-shaming. Girls losing to boys in athletic competitions. And screaming at Immigration and Customs Enforcement (ICE) officers.

There is something deeply troubling about the fact that a growing share of my generation (never mind all the older, liberal women who are praising its supposed virtues while marching in the streets, hosting slogan-filled signs, and screaming at anyone wearing a red hat. I kind of feel bad for Red Sox and Reds fans) is flirting with socialism. And we need to be honest enough to say it out loud. Gen Z isn't gravitating toward socialism because we've studied economic history and found Marx persuasive; we're gravitating toward it because we're exhausted, anxious, and staring down a future that feels increasingly out of reach.

In an interview with Tucker Carlson in August 2025, Charlie Kirk told us all what was going on with the anxiousness of young Americans and what many are doing about it.

Charlie Kirk: "The rise of Mamdani, should be a, it's a coming attraction of what's coming next."

Tucker Carlson: "Who's Mamdani?"

Kirk: "Zohran Mamdani, the Muslim communist who is running for mayor in New York City . . . most people are missing the point of what this is. This is yet another distress signal by young people to say, hey, 'If you are not going to fix our life, economically, we are going to get very radical politically. . . .

"One of the reasons [Donald Trump] was able to win younger voters, and younger men, especially, in big numbers, is that they were trying to get their leader's attention. They said, hey, this guy Donald Trump, he is pledging to go fix our economic anxiety, he is loud, he is going to get your attention. Donald Trump was a distress signal by a lot of young people, especially young men, that were stuck in a credit-centric renter economy . . . and the rise of Mamdani is just another iteration of this, only from the Left."[5]

Blaming the system is easy. Fighting against it is hard.

The political earthquake in 2025 that sent a barely known, self-described democratic socialist all the way to the mayor's office of New York City was not a fluke. Instead, it was a symptom of something far larger happening across America. What was once a small fringe called "The Squad"—an informal association of loud progressives in the Democratic Party, including Alexandria Ocasio-Cortez of New York, Ilhan Omar of Minnesota, Ayanna Pressley of Massachusetts, and Rashida Tlaib of Michigan—is now central to the future of the Democratic Party in America.

Initially just outcasts, relegated to just holding tiny press conferences screaming their hatred of America on CSPAN, the group has crept squarely into the mainstream through the doors of the mayor's mansion. The Associated Press reported, "A new Gallup poll finds that while U.S. adults overall are more likely to have a positive view of capitalism than socialism, Democrats feel differently. According to the survey, only 42% of Democrats view capitalism favorably, while 66% have a positive view of socialism."[6] Polls from 2025 show that a majority of Democratic voters now prefer democratic socialism to capitalism when each is defined, and among young Americans, the appeal of socialist ideas far outpaces confidence in traditional capitalism. In a November 2025 Axios survey, a striking 67 percent of college students said they hold a positive or neutral association with the word "socialism," compared with only 40 percent for capitalism, driven not by ideology for its own sake but by real economic anxieties, rent, healthcare, inflation, and affordability that feel unconquerable by the status quo.[7]

When you're told every day that you'll never afford a home, never pay off debt, and never start a family without two incomes and side hustles, the promise of "free" everything starts to sound like compassion instead of control. Socialism doesn't sell itself with spreadsheets; it sells itself with emotions. It dangles relief in front of a generation that feels squeezed, overlooked, and burned by institutions that overpromised and underdelivered.

We are lonely. We are broke. We are scared. And, in that fear, we are screaming at the top of our lungs, looking for someone to save us. And for many who grew up without a Bible or prayer in school, it is very common to demand that the government save us. But here is the good news: no government is coming to save you. That's not depressing; that's empowering. We have the power to shape our future, not only for ourselves but for our families, communities, and countries, thanks to the American way of thinking, that is, our American Republic and the capitalist economic structure that undergirds our success.

History is brutally consistent on this point: when government promises to be your provider, it eventually becomes your master. China, Vietnam, Poland, Germany, Russia, Cuba, and Venezuela all stand as signposts, telling us not to go the way of socialism and its evil sibling communism. Yet for all the warnings, there are many in America who refuse to believe the warning: What starts as help ends as dependence, and what begins as fairness ends in force. Every socialist system tells the same lie: that prosperity can be redistributed without first being created, that incentives don't matter, that human nature will suddenly change if the right people are in charge. They never do.

The question we must all ask is, "Have any of these ideas ever produced widespread human flourishing and economic vitality?" No! All of these ideas are rooted in selfish ambition and vain pride. And all of them have been tested and failed. Margaret Thatcher rightfully noted that "The problem with socialism is you eventually run out of other people's money."[8] Ronald Regan is widely attributed as having said, "Socialism only works in two places: heaven, where they don't need it, and hell, where they already have it." But we still want it here on Earth. Why?

Socialism doesn't fail because the wrong people implement it; it fails because it misunderstands people altogether.

Socialism doesn't fail because the wrong people implement it; it fails because it misunderstands people altogether. It trades responsibility for resentment, work for entitlement, and freedom for false security. And the cruel irony is this: the very generation being told socialism will save them is the one that will inherit the shortages, the stagnation, and the loss of opportunity that always follow.

We are being blinded by the short-term sugar rush of "free" things without being told the long-term cost of higher taxes, fewer choices, slower innovation, and a government powerful enough to give you everything, which means that it is powerful enough to take everything away. But here's the hopeful part, and it matters: Gen Z is not evil, lazy, or doomed. We are searching. We are asking real questions. And that means we are persuadable. The answer to socialism is not mockery or moral superiority; it's truth, courage, and a better vision, a vision that says dignity comes from work, not dependence.

That opportunity is expanded by freedom, not centralized power. That compassion doesn't require coercion. And the American system, while imperfect, remains the greatest engine for human flourishing the world has ever known when paired with responsibility, faith, and moral clarity. Throughout the years, many have summarized it perfectly, in one variation or another: "Capitalism is the worst economic system, except for all the others that have been tried."

My generation doesn't need a government to replace God, parents, or purpose. We need leaders willing to tell us the truth—that nothing worth having is free, that sacrifice precedes success, and that the future is not something handed to us, but something we are called to build. We need to learn to be content driving five-year-old cars and living in 2,000-square-foot starter homes. We need to stop demanding that someone else work to pay for our education. We need to show up when invited to conversations, and we need to leave our megaphones at home when we want to have a conversation with someone else.

Our public discourse is loud but incoherent. Everyone is shouting, but few are saying anything meaningful. Words are stripped of definition and inflated beyond recognition. Violence no longer means violence. Hate no longer means hate. Safety no longer means safety. Conversation becomes impossible when language itself is unstable, because without shared definitions, there is no shared reality.

Real conversation depends on clarity. It requires people to say what they mean and mean what they say. It requires the humility to listen and the confidence to respond. It assumes that truth exists and human beings are capable of approaching it together, even if imperfectly. That assumption is deeply Christian, deeply American, and deeply threatening to any system that depends on control, which is why it has been systematically dismantled.

When Screaming Counts for Something

Screaming does not equal talking. That may sound obvious, but it is one of the most important distinctions we have lost. Screaming is an emotional release. It is catharsis. It feels powerful in the moment because it overwhelms rather than persuades. Conversation, by contrast, requires discipline. It forces you to slow down, to choose your words carefully, and to risk being challenged. Screaming demands submission. Conversation invites response. Our culture increasingly rewards the former and punishes the latter.

Social media amplifies outrage because outrage is easy to consume and hard to ignore. It trains people to speak in absolutes and listen in bad faith. Cable news thrives on conflict because conflict keeps viewers engaged. Universities reward ideological alignment because alignment is easier to manage than debate. All of these incentives push in the same direction: away from conversation and toward coercion.

When we stop talking to each other, in person, at a coffee shop with classical music filling the room, we lose our sense of kindness and politeness. In restaurants, I've heard parents encourage their children to "use their inside voices," and in church, I've watched grandparents tell their grandkids to "stop fidgeting and sit still." But I've never heard anyone tell someone online to "use your loving voice."

Social media, for all of its fun when it is used to celebrate family, promote charities, encourage prayer, share hobbies, and organize like-minded efforts, is also a dark place of cyberbullying, addiction, fear of missing out, and doxxing. For example, the Cyberbullying Research Center conducted research and found that "approximately 55% of the students in our 2023 sample reported that they experienced cyberbullying at some point in their lifetimes. About 27% said they had been cyberbullied in the most recent 30 days. When asked about specific types of cyberbullying experienced in the previous 30 days, mean or hurtful comments posted online (30.4%), exclusion from group chats (28.9%), rumors spread online (28.4%), and someone embarrassing or humiliating them online (26.9%) were the most commonly-reported."[9] I would bet that the same people who yell and scream and bully online would be much less likely to do so sitting across the table in a coffee shop with the same person.

Why are we not encouraging each other to talk more? And listen even more? Why are we so afraid to have our ideas challenged, our emotions hurt, and our worldviews shaken? Do we really believe the little bubbles we live in are the best bubbles for us? Can we not see that by avoiding intellectually and emotionally stimulating conversations, we are creating prisons for ourselves and perpetuating the very loneliness we are trying to avoid, without social media addictions?

If only there were a place where young minds—say, those of young men and women between the ages of, oh, I don't know, eighteen to twenty-two—could go and interact with their peers and older men and women who care about them enough to teach them how to reason and debate. How to listen and adapt. How to experience new and beautiful things and to manage their emotions better than they did in their adolescence. If only.

Public Education Is Failing Children and the Country

Sorry, not sorry, if this offends you, but public education in modern-day America is the equivalent of taxpayer-funded obedience training, all bent away from God and toward the Marxist ideologues who seek to undo America and the Christian religion that shaped it. And this effort has been training us to avoid interacting with people who we suppose believe or behave differently than we do.

> ***Sorry, not sorry if this offends you, but public education in modern-day America is the equivalent of taxpayer-funded obedience training.***

According to political communication scholars, while Americans are still talking about politics, those conversations increasingly happen within ideologically homogeneous circles rather than across viewpoints, meaning disagreement has shrunk even while total discussion has grown. Moreover, a 2025 Foundation for Individual Rights and Expression (FIRE) survey of over sixty-eight thousand college students found that a majority now oppose inviting controversial speakers to campus, regardless of ideology, and only 28 percent of students believe it is never acceptable to shout down a speaker, while many students even believe disruptive or violent protest tactics can be acceptable.[10] Self-censorship and avoidance of politically sensitive topics are also widespread, illustrating how conversation has been replaced by disengagement or conflict avoidance rather than genuine dialogue.

The tragedy is that most people do not actually want this. They want to be heard. They want to be understood. They want to have their concerns taken seriously without being mocked or dismissed. But wanting conversation and knowing how to participate in it are not the same thing. Many people have never been taught how to argue without dehumanizing others, how to listen without surrendering their identity, or how to speak with conviction without becoming cruel.

So, they retreat. Or they lash out. Or they perform.

We are too easily offended. What if the goal was to have an unoffendable heart? What if we gave others the benefit of the doubt when we bump up against differing viewpoints? What if we prayed for those who stand against us?

The problem for Gen Z is that we have been dropped into an environment that punishes curiosity and rewards conformity, primarily in schools and on social media. And we have not yet learned how to talk ourselves out of the problem.

This is where the lost art of conversation becomes most obvious. Conversation used to be understood as a skill. It had rules, norms, and expectations. You listened before responding. You addressed arguments rather than real or perceived motives. You allowed room for disagreement without assuming bad faith. Those norms were not perfect, but they provided a framework that made persuasion possible. Today, those guardrails are gone, or they have been replaced.

And here we have the big problem. Because we have been told to "shut up and sit down," and to "trust the science," and have been called "racists" over and over again by voices on the Left, instead of asking whether something is true, we ask whether it is acceptable. Instead of responding to arguments, we assign labels. Instead of engaging people, we manage optics. The goal is no longer understanding but insulation. And once insulation becomes the priority, conversation becomes a liability.

That shift has enormous consequences for our democratic republic. Self-government assumes that citizens can reason together. It assumes that people with different interests and beliefs can argue, compromise, and coexist without resorting to force. When conversation collapses, that assumption collapses with it. Politics becomes a zero-sum contest of power rather than a process of persuasion. That is when everything hardens.

You can see it in how people talk past each other rather than to each other.

"How are you doing?" Keep walking.

"Good, how are you?" Keep walking.

"Good." Keep walking.

You can see it in how debates turn into shouting matches. You can see it in how quickly disagreements escalate into moral condemnations. The loss of conversation does not just make us less polite. It makes us less capable of resolving conflict without domination.

And domination is always someone's end goal.

This is why we find ourselves "walking in the fear of man," which is a snare, according to one of the wisest men to ever live.[1] How can we engage in meaningful conversation and debate when we are held captive by others' opinions? How can we learn without exchanging ideas with others?

President John F. Kennedy once reminded the nation that "without debate, without criticism, no administration and no country can succeed,"[11] yet we now treat disagreement as cultural and political sabotage rather than the lifeblood of the future of our country. We confuse peace with quiet and unity with compliance, as if the absence of argument

1. Proverbs 29:25.

means the presence of health. In reality, a society that cannot tolerate criticism becomes brittle. When conversation disappears, persuasion gives way to power, and power rarely feels obligated to explain itself once questioning is no longer allowed. The death of conversation is not a social inconvenience; it is a political warning sign.

C. S. Lewis warned decades ago that reason is "the natural organ of truth,"[12] which explains why modern culture works so hard to avoid it. Reason demands patience. It demands humility. It demands the willingness to lose an argument in pursuit of something higher than ego. None of those virtues thrives in an outrage economy. When conversation collapses, truth does not automatically rise to the top. The loudest voice does, and volume has never been a substitute for wisdom.

Conversation is threatening precisely because it humanizes. It makes us less lonely and less dependent on a government thousands of miles away. It invites us to belong somewhere other than online. It calms our nerves by helping us feel heard and understood (well, at least it can, if done correctly.) It forces us to confront the fact that the person across from us is not a caricature or an enemy but a human being with reasons for believing what they believe.

You may still disagree. You may disagree deeply. But once you recognize the humanity of the other person, certain tactics become harder to justify.

That is why authoritarian systems always attack conversation first. They do not begin by banning speech outright. They undermine the norms that make speech meaningful. They flood the public square with noise. They blur definitions.

They incentivize outrage. And eventually, people lose the ability to distinguish between screaming and talking. At that point, force becomes inevitable.

This is where our politics has gone off the rails. We no longer feel comfortable talking to each other. We no longer see disagreement as an opportunity to learn or persuade but as an excuse to dominate. The goal is not to change minds but to crush opposition. That posture may feel satisfying in the short term, but it is corrosive over time. A movement that cannot persuade will eventually be forced to coerce, and coercion always comes with a cost that freedom cannot afford. Conversation is the only alternative.

That is why Scripture places such an emphasis on how we should live with, think about, and behave toward one another. We need to learn to "Be at peace with each other,"[1] "Stop passing judgment on one another,"[2] "Pray for each other,"[3] "Instruct one another,"[4] "Live in harmony with one another,"[5] "Encourage one another daily,"[6] and "Carry each other's burdens."[7] If we do this, live with, think about, and behave well toward one another, we will be more comfortable talking with each other, and we will all feel a little less lonely and scream a whole lot less. And the great news is, we don't have to do it alone.

---

1. Mark 9:50.
2. Romans 14:13.
3. James 5:16.
4. Romans 15:14.
5. 1 Peter 3:8
6. Hebrews 3:13.
7. Galatians 6:2.

One of the most damaging lies of our time is that conversation requires the compromise of principle. That to listen is to surrender. That to engage is to legitimize. This lie thrives in environments where outrage is currency and where admitting complexity exists is seen as betrayal. But conversation does not demand agreement. It demands honesty. It demands the confidence to say, "This is what I believe, and here is why," without turning the other person into an enemy.

That kind of engagement is harder than shouting slogans or posting hot takes. It requires preparation. It requires patience. It requires the willingness to lose an argument without losing your integrity. And it requires a belief that the person you are talking to is capable of reason, even if they are currently wrong. That belief is foundational to both Christianity and a constitutional government rooted in self-government by *the people*.

Jesus did not call disciples who agreed with each other on everything. He called a zealot who believed violence was justified to overthrow Rome and a tax collector who worked for the very system that the zealot despised. Matthew the tax collector and Simon the Zealot did not just disagree politically. They represented opposing worldviews that had spilled real blood. Most would say that Matthew, a Jewish man who was employed as a tax collector, was beholden to the leaders of the Roman Empire for whom he worked. And Simon the Zealot, a Jewish man who was part of a faction of the people to literally assassinate the rulers of Rome, was beholden to the political ideas of the Jewish leaders. And yet Christ called both of them to walk together, to learn together, and to be transformed together.

If Jesus could do the work of discipleship in Simon, a man comfortable with radicalism and violence, then it is absurd to believe that persuasion is impossible in our own time. If He could free Matthew from the vices of money and persuade him to seek first the Kingdom of God and not the gifts or Rome, He could do the same with us.

Let us live together, one another, talking and listening and laughing and growing and healing and working and playing. Don't believe it's possible? Let's talk about it. And to the older generations reading this, people my parents' and grandparents' age, let me say something from the heart. My generation doesn't need you to lecture us from across the room or dismiss us as kids who don't understand the world yet. What we want is a seat at the table. We want to be heard, challenged, and taken seriously. We want mentors who will listen before they instruct and guide before they criticize.

Most of us aren't looking for a fight with the generations that came before us. We're looking for partners who care enough about the future of this country to talk with us, not just about us.

If you're willing to do that, you may be surprised how ready Gen Z is to listen, learn, and carry forward what you've built.

PART III
WHAT MUST BE DONE

Chapter 7
The Courage to Disagree and Be Booed

Some said I had been brave. That is nonsense. Anyone who says he has never felt fear is a liar. It was not so much a question of courage as of experience.[1]

—Richard Nixon

It takes little courage to remain silent. If you refuse to speak, you don't step outside the moment; you surrender it to whoever is loudest, cruelest, and most willing to take power. In moments that decide history, neutrality is not innocence. It's abdication.

As it relates to American politics, I don't understand Independents. I mean, I do—it's just that sometimes I want to scream, "Pick a side!" I hear a lot of people say there is not much of a difference between the Left and the Right in America. Others say the "one-party system" is to blame. But for me, there is an ocean of difference between what Democrats want to do to America and what Republicans want to save America from. If you don't know the difference, Republicans, at least the conservative ones, want to maintain as much of God's law, natural law, moral law, and the intent of the American Founders as possible, believing that this is right and good and noble. Democrats, especially the progressive ones, say they want to redeem America from its sins and move as quickly as possible away from the founding era and any Christian language that might have been present in it. As G. K. Chesterton said, "The whole modern world has divided itself into Conservatives and Progressives. The business of Progressives is to go on making mistakes. The business of Conservatives is to prevent mistakes from being corrected."[2]

But here is the lie that prevents many from doing so: neutrality. It is a lie at the center of modern American life, and it is one of the most destructive lies our generation has inherited. Independence does not remove you from the equation; it justifies silence. When you refuse to speak, refuse to vote, refuse to engage, or refuse to testify, you are not opting out of history; you are empowering whoever already has the microphone. So, with the greatest humility I can muster, to my friends who ascribe to the supposed nobility of "independence," pick a side. Have the courage to take a position, defend it, listen to opposing viewpoints, and adapt as needed. Be willing to be booed by those who disagree with you, rather than trying to appease everyone and appeal to no one.

They tell us Gen Z is soft. Entitled. Ashamed of America. But in 2024, during anti-Israel protests that spread onto college campuses across the country, when the American flag was ripped down at the University of North Carolina, stomped on, and replaced with a political banner, a group of fraternity guys decided they'd had enough.[3] While activists screamed and objects flew, these young men walked into the chaos, picked up the flag, and held it in the air so it wouldn't touch the ground. No PR team. No scripted virtue signal. Just instinct. Just conviction. They understood something the loudest voices on campus seemed to forget: that flag represents more than politics. It represents sacrifice, graves, families, and freedoms paid for in blood. And while others were busy trying to tear down the country that gave them the right to protest, these guys stood there and physically held it up. That wasn't privilege. That was courage. That wasn't hate. That was loyalty. And it proved something the media doesn't want to admit—there is a rising generation that refuses to bow to cultural intimidation. You can mock them, cancel them, or call them names. But you can't call them cowards.

The late Supreme Court Justice Antonin Scalia, the greatest justice to sit on the bench so far, didn't sugarcoat what real conviction looks like. He warned believers, "Have the courage to have your wisdom regarded as stupidity. Be fools for Christ. And have the courage to suffer the contempt of the sophisticated world."[4] That's the line our culture keeps trying to erase. Today, the pressure isn't just to disagree with faith or traditional values. It's to laugh at them, shame them, and push them out of public life entirely. The goal is simple: Make standing for truth feel embarrassing enough that people stop doing it. But Scalia understood something timeless: Every generation that holds to truth gets called foolish by the one drifting away from it. The real danger isn't being mocked by the cultural elites; it's surrendering just to avoid their approval ratings. If we actually want a country that can talk again, instead of one where everyone quietly caves to the loudest voices, it's going to take people willing to stand firm, take the hits, and keep speaking anyway.

Every generation faces moments where silence feels safer than speech and then, later, explains how it "didn't know" things would go this far. But history does not accept ignorance as innocence. The record is clear: what people tolerate quietly shapes what their children must confront loudly. Silence compounds. It doesn't end conflicts; it delays them until they're more expensive.

Every moral moment has gravity. It pulls. It aligns. It forces outcomes whether you participate consciously or not. The idea that you can hover above the moment, detached and unaffected, is a luxury fiction sold to people who want the benefits of citizenship without the burden of responsibility. In reality, history does not pause while you decide whether to get involved. It moves forward, shaped by those willing to act. You weren't born to spectate your own future. And if you dare to ask questions and share ideas, you will be remembered; maybe not right away. You need to risk being called a crank, curmudgeon, or malcontent. You need to be willing to be booed off stage. Meaningful debate, and the future of America, demands nothing less.

When people of conviction go quiet, people of chaos do not. This is not a theory. It is an observable fact. Loud minorities dominate silent majorities every time. Not because they are more numerous, but because they are present. Power flows toward participation. Always has, always will. Silence doesn't weaken bad ideas; it clears the runway for them.

Now, you don't get to abandon the field and complain about who won. American Christians talk like a moral majority and vote like a disengaged minority. For decades, Christians have described themselves as a moral majority. In practice, they have behaved like a disengaged minority. Voter turnout among self-identified evangelicals regularly lags behind their rhetorical influence. A 2024 survey revealed that "among those are people who are defined by their beliefs regarding sin and salvation as born-again Christians (41 million expected to not vote); self-identified Christians who regularly attend church services (32 million not expected to vote); and voting-age adults who regularly attend an evangelical church (14 million of whom are expected to not vote). The research also indicated 46 million adults who attend Protestant churches and 19 million who attend Catholic churches are not likely to vote."[5] And voting is the absolute lowest and easiest form of political debate because it is done in secret! But even worse, sermons address cultural decay rather than civic responsibility, and congregations pray for leaders they did not help elect, then lament policies they did not attempt to stop.

This withdrawal is often spiritualized. Politics is framed as "worldly." Engagement is dismissed as divisive. Silence is mistaken for humility. But the effect is not neutrality; it is surrender. Laws are written, institutions are shaped, and norms are enforced regardless of whether Christians participate. Abstention does not pause outcomes; it guarantees others will decide them.

History doesn't remember who played it safe. More specifically, history has never rewarded believers who retreat from public responsibility. Faith has always lived in tension with power. When Christians abandon the civic arena, they don't preserve holiness; they outsource influence. Evil rarely needs your agreement. It only needs your quiet.

Evil rarely needs your agreement. It only needs your quiet.

I remember sitting in a classroom where the conversation slowly drifted into politics—not formally, not as a debate, just casually, the way it always does when people feel safe assuming everyone agrees. A professor made an offhand comment that earned a few nods and a couple of laughs. Nothing outrageous. Nothing that would make headlines. But something I fundamentally disagreed with. I felt that familiar tightening in my chest, the moment where you weigh truth against comfort. I looked around the room and realized I wasn't just deciding whether to speak. I was deciding whether I was willing to be *seen*.

I didn't raise my hand. Not because I didn't know what to say. Not because I was unsure. But because I knew exactly what would happen next: the tone shift, the subtle eye-rolling, the way silence would follow me for the rest of the semester. I walked out of class that day realizing something unsettling: silence had become the expected posture, not the exception. And the cost of speaking wasn't theoretical; it was social, academic, relational.

Scripture is brutally honest about this. There is no category for moral neutrality in the Bible: There are those who act in obedience and those who don't. Those who speak and those who withhold. Those who stand watch and those who look away. The consequences differ, but the responsibility does not. In the Book of Proverbs, God proclaims, "If you say, 'But we knew nothing about this,' does not he who weighs the heart perceive it? Does not he who guards your life know it? Will he not repay everyone according to what they have done?"[1]

Elie Wiesel, in his 1986 acceptance speech for the Nobel Peace Prize, expressed that he understood neutrality better than most when he said, "Neutrality helps the oppressor, never the victim."[6] Dietrich Bonhoeffer went even further, insisting that "silence in the face of evil is itself evil."[7] His words leave no room to hide. Silence is not innocence. It is alignment. And alignment carries responsibility.

Jesus never entertained the fantasy of neutrality or silence. He forced alignment, saying, "Follow me,"[2] and "No

1. Proverbs 24:12.
2. Matthew 4:19; Mark 8:34; Luke 9:29 John 12:26.

one can serve two masters."[1] That is the choice in front of us now.

Debating Whether Christians Should Join the Debate

The importance of debate cannot be overstated. Within a single conversation, there can be a mutually beneficial exchange of arguments. Critical thinking can be developed. The art of persuasion grows. And if the debate goes on long enough with sincerity, the participants and observers can learn to analyze complex topics from multiple perspectives. Moving people beyond silence, reasoned debate empowers people and affirms or challenges their current viewpoints. And, if approached with love and truth, it can help us mature and succeed. Maybe we are comfortable doing this at work, but what about at home? Or in a Bible study? Or with others who may or may not intend to vote?

We tell ourselves stories to justify avoiding debate: "I'm not smart enough." "I don't want anyone's feelings to get hurt." "Politics is messy." "I don't like either side." "My faith is personal." "I don't want to be divisive." What we rarely admit is the truth: Participation costs something, and silence feels easier. Silence preserves comfort. Silence avoids tension. Silence allows you to feel morally intact without doing anything that might actually risk something.

Thinking again about politics and our country, every election that is decided by razor-thin margins is a referendum on silence. Every school board that is overtaken by activists

---

1. Luke 16:13.

because parents stayed home is a monument to cowardice. Every institution that is captured by the Left occurs not because the majority wanted it, but because they did not publicly object to it. Outcomes are shaped not only by those who push aggressively, but by those who quietly step aside.

Silence votes for whoever shows up. When you don't speak, you authorize whoever already has the microphone.

Gen Z is inheriting institutions shaped not by the convictions of the majority, but by the activism of the committed minority. Campuses, classrooms, corporate culture, and even churches did not transform overnight. Still, the silent majority who have been leading them have been surrendering these institutions to the minority, because they were and are afraid to tell the truth, for a whole variety of reasons, and with many reasoned justifications, I'm sure.

> ***When you don't speak, you authorize whoever already has the microphone.***

Every system rewards participation. Those who show up decide. Those who stay home surrender influence. And those who are willing to debate often win, because victory goes to the one who has the courage to show up. This is not cynical. It is structural.

Now, I know this chapter has a lot of words directed at Christians. For those of you who like the ideas of a young Republican but are not yet engaged with a church or Jesus Himself, thanks for hanging in there with me. I keep talking to my fellow churchgoers, because for a long time, we've been told that Christians are supposed to be loving and kind.

That we should "take the high road" and be quick to forgive. That we should turn the other cheek. And all of these things are true. But we have not been told that there is a world of lies crushing kids, one generation after the next, and we can and must do something about it. When Christians disengage from civic life under the banner of spiritual purity, they do not keep politics clean or kids safe. They hand it and them over to those intent on abusing them. And once it is handed over, reclaiming them becomes far more costly.

So, this chapter is my first volley in the discussion—the debate, if you will. I am willing to be booed. I am willing to have some of you close this book and unfollow me. Why? Because low-propensity voting among Christians is not a mystery. It is a theology problem disguised as a turnout problem. Some have been taught that faith and public life must remain separate, that engagement compromises holiness, and that involvement signals misplaced allegiance. But Scripture does not support that withdrawal.

Romans 13 is often cited to argue for disengagement or passive submission (and those of you who argue this, you know who you are), but that reading misses the point. Authority is acknowledged, not deified. Government is described as a servant, not a savior. Obedience is never portrayed as blind silence.

When Christians opt out of voting, disengage from school boards, avoid local governance, and retreat from public conversations, they are not preserving the faith. They are shrinking it. Faith that never confronts power becomes sentiment. Belief that never risks consequences becomes decoration.

Gen Z is watching this unfold in real time. They see churches preach conviction on Sunday and then disappear on Tuesday. They hear moral clarity from pulpits and then watch leaders avoid controversy when it matters. They notice the disconnect. And many conclude, consciously or not, that faith is performative rather than consequential. That conclusion is devastating.

We all know the future of America is always in the hands (and minds) of the next generations. Today, young people are not asking for perfection. They are asking for consistency. They want to know whether belief actually shapes action or whether it dissolves under pressure. Silence answers that question loudly. It communicates that comfort outranks courage and that avoiding conflict matters more than telling the truth. And historically, the silence of the church has been telling us kids there is no hope.

The Illusion That People Don't Care

One of the most misunderstood realities of modern politics is not that people don't care; it's that many are waiting for voices they can trust. In 2024, surveys showed that 89 percent of Americans worry about fake political information online—not because they're disengaged, but because they're discerning.[8] That's not apathy. That's maturity. It means people are hungry for authenticity, clarity, and leaders willing to speak plainly without manipulation or spin (thank you, Charlie).

At the same time, data shows that while not everyone posts about politics constantly, millions of Americans are still watching, listening, and forming opinions.[9] Silence online doesn't mean disengagement; it means the loudest voices don't automatically represent the majority. That creates an opening. When thoughtful, grounded people speak with conviction instead of outrage, they stand out. They lead. They set the tone.

This is the moment when silence can be replaced with stewardship. Not everyone is called to go viral. But everyone is called to be honest about where they stand. When everyday Americans choose to speak, at work, at church, at home, on campus, the culture shifts. Quiet conviction, multiplied across millions of lives, is how movements grow without losing their soul.

Choosing to stay out of the debate, out of the discussion, out of the crossfire, aligns you with those in power because power fills quiet spaces. This alignment does not require agreement; it only requires absence. Institutions do not need unanimous support to change. They need uninterrupted momentum, one absent board member at a time. When no one pushes back, policies become precedent. When no one questions assumptions, ideology hardens into dogma.

The idea that staying out of politics is "caring" or that it preserves unity is an illusion. Unity built on avoidance is fragile. It fractures the moment pressure is applied. True unity is forged through compassion, shared conviction, and honest engagement. And as long as so-called "caring Christians" remain one of the largest but quietest constituencies in the country, decisions will continue to be made without them, by the people who hate their God, and them by association.

At some point, every excuse for silence collapses under the same question: Who benefits if you stay quiet? It is never the truth. It is never the vulnerable. It is never the future. Here are a few of the excuses I've heard:

I'm Staying Out of It

"I'm staying out of it" is not a principled position. It is an excuse used by those who prefer to be entertained rather than informed. It helps those who are afraid to offend others. Ultimately, it is a decision to let others decide for you.

Christians Should Be Humble

People often justify silence by claiming humility. They say they don't want to impose their views, don't want to be divisive, don't want to be political. But humility should never refuse to speak the truth. In this case, it is self-preservation dressed up as virtue.

Jesus's Kingdom Is Not of This World

True. But all of the kingdoms of this world, and the goals they have to destroy humanity, are of Jesus's world. Human flourishing is dependent upon God's grace, which most often shows up in the lives of Christians as they follow Jesus, wherever they are.

Politics Keeps People Out of the Church

Maybe. But so does hypocrisy and the appearance of not caring enough to get involved. We can never go wrong speaking the truth in love. If someone chooses to be offended and blames you or your church or Jesus because of you, know that you are not responsible for their relationship with God. The Holy Spirit is. Trust Him.

Revelation 12:11 tells us that the people of God overcome "by the word of their testimony." Not by dominance. Not by control. By lovingly witnessing to the truth. Testimony is not an abstract belief. It is spoken allegiance. It is the truth made public. And testimony, by definition, cannot exist in silence.

Silence feels cheap now, but the bill comes later. It comes when institutions no longer reflect the values people claim to hold. It comes when children are educated by ideologies their parents never challenged. It comes when churches lose moral authority because they avoid moral moments in society. It comes when culture shifts so far that speaking feels impossible, not because speech was forbidden, but because it was abandoned.

That pattern is repeating itself, and Gen Z is standing in the crosshairs. This generation will either inherit a culture shaped by conviction or one surrendered by apathy. There is no neutral inheritance. What is left undefended will be redefined. What is left unspoken will be rewritten. And what is left unattended will be taken over.

Every time you choose not to speak, not to vote, not to engage, and not to testify, you are not stepping outside the moment. You are shaping it. You are casting a vote for inertia. You are allowing momentum to move unchecked. And momentum, once established, is far harder to stop than it is to challenge early.

Christians cannot claim surprise at the direction of culture while refusing to participate in the moments that shaped it. Faith that never leaves the sanctuary will not survive the public square. Belief that never risks consequences will eventually lose credibility.

You do not get to stay "neutral." God cares too much for you not to engage. Scripture makes this distinction explicit: "For God has not given us a spirit of fear, but of power and of love and of a sound mind."[1] Christians know that God does not give His people a spirit of fear, but of power, love, and a sound mind. That triad matters. Power without love becomes tyranny. Love without power becomes sentimentality. And without a sound mind, neither can be exercised rightly. Courage, biblically understood, is not recklessness or aggression. It is clarity under pressure. It is steadiness when the emotional temperature rises. It is the refusal to surrender truth simply because it has become unpopular. And what is really unpopular today? Love without truth is not love at all.

The Courage to Be Booed

If you've never been booed, you probably haven't said anything that mattered. Truth doesn't glide through history on standing ovations; it limps forward through rejection. Every meaningful reformer was called dangerous before they were called right. The boos are not a sign you failed; they're often proof you finally hit something real.

There is a moment every person eventually faces when conviction collides with consequence. It is the point where belief stops being theoretical and starts demanding something from you. Until that moment arrives, courage feels abstract. It is easy to praise boldness when it is distant and easy

1. 2 Timothy 1:7.

to cheer when someone else is paying the price. But when the room turns, when the applause dies, when approval gives way to resistance, courage reveals its true cost. That is the moment most people avoid

It was the summer of 2024, my first book had just come out, and I had flown back from a New York City media tour that morning, still half-unpacked, already repacking to head to Milwaukee the next day to meet with President Trump's team and help prepare content creators for the RNC convention. It was one of those days where adrenaline hadn't worn off yet, when your phone hasn't stopped buzzing in weeks, and you're trying to remember what normal feels like.

I had the news on, which showed President Trump speaking during a rally in Butler, Pennsylvania, while I hopped on a call with some high school buddies to catch up, laughing about golf scores and the latest drama. I muted the TV, leaned back, and for a moment, everything felt ordinary.

Then my phone started shaking. Not buzzing. Not lighting up. Shaking. Notifications stacked so fast my screen couldn't keep up. "Pray for Trump." "Is this real?" "Please tell me you're seeing this." Over and over again. I remember pulling the phone away from my ear mid-sentence and unmuting the television. The podium was empty.

Secret Service agents were scrambling across the stage. People were screaming. And in that instant, before any official confirmation, before any anchor said a word, I knew exactly what had happened. I didn't think; I reacted. I dropped to my knees on the living room floor and prayed. Not a polished prayer. Not a political prayer. Just, "God, please. Please."

I yelled to my family, who quickly joined me in front of the TV. For what seemed like an hour, but was in fact just seconds, there was nothing but chaos. And then we saw him. Donald Trump stood up. Blood on his face. Fist in the air.

I remember turning to my dad, my voice steady in a moment that didn't deserve steadiness, and saying, "If he survives this, he just won the election."

Not because of sympathy, but because history recognizes courage when it shows itself unfiltered, unscripted, and unafraid. This was his Teddy Roosevelt moment. This was the moment we saw the courage of the legend, and he embodied the clarity of Roosevelt when he said,

> It is not the critic who counts: not the man who points out how the strong man stumbles or where the doer of deeds could have done better. The credit belongs to the man who is actually in the arena, whose face is marred by dust and sweat and blood, who strives valiantly, who errs and comes up short again and again, because there is no effort without error or shortcoming, but who knows the great enthusiasms, the great devotions, who spends himself in a worthy cause; who, at the best, knows, in the end, the triumph of high achievement, and who, at the worst, if he fails, at least he fails while daring greatly, so that his place shall never be with those cold and timid souls who knew neither victory nor defeat.[10]

The man in the arena, literally bleeding, refusing to retreat. In an age obsessed with safety, optics, and curated narratives, the image of a leader standing back up after someone tried to kill him cut through the noise in a way no speech ever could.

But here's the part most people miss: That moment wasn't just about Trump. It was about what happens when rhetoric turns people into monsters, and disagreement turns into dehumanization. When speech is treated as violence long enough, *violence eventually follows*. A culture that teaches people their political opponents are existential threats will eventually produce someone willing to act like it.

That day hardened something in me.

I already understood the stakes of speaking out. I'd already read death threats. I'd already had security briefings. But watching an assassination attempt unfold in real time forced a deeper realization: this isn't theoretical anymore. The loss of civil discourse doesn't just poison relationships; it puts blood on the ground.

And yet, even then, what stood out wasn't fear. It was resolve.

Trump didn't whisper after that day. He didn't retreat into silence. He didn't apologize for existing. He stood taller. And in doing so, he reminded the country, and my generation, of something we've forgotten: history doesn't belong to the cautious. It belongs to the courageous.

I know that some people think I am an "old soul," or that I quote Ronald Reagan too much, and some of them even make fun of me for sounding like I'm stuck in the nineties (I was born in 2006). I take that as a sign that I am doing something right. One of my favorite songs is on the 1970 album *The Fightin' Side of Me* by Merle Haggard. I bet most of you have never heard of it. But I can say that, after I started getting death threats, I made it my walkout song. Now, every crowd I speak to hears the song and understands that those who seek to tear down America are walking on the fighting side of me.

A Modern-Day Teddy Roosevelt

Who exemplified that better than the man who taught my generation how to talk to each other? He was murdered by someone who believed silencing his opponent was easier than debating him.

Charlie Kirk never feared disagreement. He feared what would happen when disagreement disappeared. Long before the country recognized the danger we were drifting toward, he warned me that the extinction of civil discourse would not lead to peace; it would lead to chaos. And he was right.

Charlie went to the places no one else would go. He stood in front of hostile crowds, got heckled and booed, answered every question, and modeled something almost extinct in American life: the belief that people with radically different views could still speak to one another without violence. That belief cost him his life.

The irony is unbearable. The man demonized for years as "dangerous" was killed by a culture that no longer knows how to argue.

After his death, I thought about how easy it would be to step back. To lower my voice. To decide that the cost of speaking wasn't worth paying. But the question that haunted me wasn't whether speaking was dangerous; it was whether silence was faithful.

Charlie didn't live cautiously. He lived obediently. He understood that courage is not the absence of fear, but the decision to speak anyway. His legacy is not a brand or an organization. It is a standard: show up, take questions, speak clearly, and never surrender conversation to intimidation.

If we honor him at all, it must be by refusing to retreat into silence.

William F. Buckley Jr. famously described a conservative as the person who stands "athwart history, yelling 'Stop,' "[11] not because movement is always wrong, but because momentum is not morality. Every era rushes somewhere. Someone has to ask whether that direction is good, true, or sustainable. And that person is almost never applauded in real time. They are mocked first, marginalized next, and vindicated only later, if history is generous. Booing is often the price of clarity in a confused age.

Every meaningful advance in truth has required people who are willing to endure disapproval. A boo does not automatically mean you are wrong. Sometimes, it means you are early. Sometimes, it means you are challenging a lie that has grown comfortable. Sometimes, it means you have spoken clearly in a room that depends on confusion. And sometimes it means you need to refine your argument or your tone. A sound mind is required to tell the difference.

Every meaningful advance in truth has required people who are willing to endure disapproval.

We have confused courage with volume and fearlessness with cruelty. We have celebrated those who provoke reaction without substance and dismissed those who speak calmly in hostile environments. The result is a culture that is loud but brittle, confident but shallow, bold in appearance and fragile in reality.

The courage to be booed is different. It is not about seeking opposition for its own sake. It is about refusing to let opposition dictate belief. It is about standing still long enough to be misunderstood without panicking. It is about trusting that truth does not require unanimous consent to remain true.

That kind of courage is rare because it can't be faked. You can't perform it convincingly for long. It reveals itself under pressure, when incentives flip, and the cost becomes real.

The first time a room turns on you, it feels disorienting. Your body reacts before your mind catches up. Your heart rate jumps. Your thoughts race. You replay every sentence, wondering which word crossed the line and whether there is still time to pull it back. That moment reveals how deeply approval has been wired into us as a measure of safety. Being booed triggers the same instinct as physical danger because, for most of human history, rejection from the group actually was dangerous. Our brains have not caught up to the modern world, and fear exploits that lag.

Jerry Seinfeld, as only he can do, sheds a bit of light on this topic of sharing our ideas and speaking in public: "According to most studies, people's number one fear is public speaking. Number two is death. Death is number two. Does that sound right? This means to the average person, if you go to a funeral, you're better off in the casket than doing the eulogy."[12]

I get it. I, too, get nervous before speaking engagements. I wonder how people are going to view me, think of me, and whether they will curse at me from across the quad for something I say. But still, I have to do it. This is the courage of my conviction. I must do my part because I asked God to send me, and He did. I know I'm going to get booed, but I can't let that stop me.

The courage to be booed cannot be outsourced or crowdsourced. You cannot borrow it from a movement or inherit it from a platform. It has to be forged in moments where retreat would be easier, and silence would be safer. Hostility exposes motives. When applause disappears, you find out why you were speaking in the first place. If affirmation was the fuel, the tank empties quickly. If conviction was the fuel, you keep going. That distinction becomes clearer with each encounter. Some people respond to boos by hardening into bitterness. Others respond by collapsing into silence. Both reactions miss the point.

The goal is not to enjoy being booed. The goal is to remain steady when it happens. This steadiness is what separates leaders from performers. Performers need the room with them. Leaders can move ahead of it. Performers adjust their message to solicit a desired reaction. Leaders refine their message to align with the truth. The difference is not personality. It is character and conviction.

> ***The goal is not to enjoy being booed. The goal is to remain steady when it happens.***

Our culture's relationship with political expression is becoming more fraught, and in some respects, more dangerous. Why? I think it is because we lack the courage to debate or be booed.

Recent surveys indicate that nearly half of college students now believe it is acceptable to block access to controversial speakers or even shout them down, with a growing minority reporting that, in some situations, using force to stop speech is justified. A 2025 YouGov poll showed that 19 percent of adults under thirty say political violence can sometimes be justified, compared with 11 percent overall, revealing a generational shift in tolerance for extreme responses to speech.[13] Younger Americans increasingly distrust both major parties and believe the country is headed in the wrong direction, illustrating how frustration and polarization shape their willingness to engage, or resist, controversial expression. That realization strips fear of much of its power.

In 1985, a Dallas pastor named W. A. Criswell stood before the Southern Baptist Convention and delivered a warning that still hits today. He said that "whether we live or die . . . depends upon our attitude to the Word of God."[14] In other words, the future isn't decided by our slogans or how comfortable we feel. It's decided by whether we actually stand when it counts. Every generation gets its moment where staying quiet feels easier than speaking up, where going along with the culture feels safer than holding the line. This is ours. Nations don't usually lose themselves in one dramatic collapse; they lose themselves when normal people slowly decide the fight for truth isn't worth the cost. The real question isn't whether pressure will come. It's whether we'll still have the courage to stand when it does.

Courage in these moments does not mean escalating conflict. It means refusing to mirror chaos. It means staying calm, speaking clearly, and treating others as capable of reason, even when they are not acting like it. It means speaking the truth in love. It means testifying to what matters to God and your neighbors.

Remember, you live for an audience of One, and the critic doesn't count. If an eleven-year-old kid can do it, so can you.

I want you to be the next Samantha Fulnecky, Teddy Roosevelt, or Charlie Kirk. I want you to have the courage to raise your hand, disagree with others (politely), and even be booed. And I'll tell you—you won't know if you have the courage to be booed until you try it. So here are a few ways you can test the waters safely to see what happens.

If you're in a group of friends, talking about something that really doesn't matter, like favorite bands or sports stars, if everyone seems to agree, then disagree and see what happens. Let your ego feel the awkwardness. When you realize that your friends are still your friends, you will gain a little more courage.

When someone shares a post online that you don't agree with, send them a private message, saying something like, "I appreciate your thoughts on the topic. While I don't fully agree, it is good to see people sharing their opinions in public." And see what happens. No matter their response, affirm your courage to say you disagree.

If someone says something ill of a politician you don't like, maybe, "Trump" or "Obama," have the courage to correct them and say, "I always like to refer to them as 'President Trump' or 'President Obama' in public, whether I disagree with them or not." Be bold and stand for courtesy in politics.

CHAPTER 8
The Moral Act of Conversation

> *With malice toward none, with charity for all . . . let us strive on . . . to achieve and cherish a just and lasting peace.*[1]
>
> —Abraham Lincoln

Outrage is cheap. It costs nothing, proves nothing, and spreads fast. The rarest form of strength in modern politics is not volume; it's restraint. There is a difference between being bold and being reckless, and our culture has spent years pretending the two are interchangeable. Loudness is praised as courage. Cruelty is excused as honesty. Outrage is mistaken for conviction. And anyone who refuses to participate in that theater is accused of weakness, cowardice, or compromise. This confusion has done real damage, not just to public discourse, but to the credibility of those who claim to care about truth. Being outspoken is necessary. Being outrageous is optional. But listening is the key to public discourse and the embracing of wisdom.

In *Mere Christianity*, C. S. Lewis explains why there is so much outrage. Not directly, but because he is offering insights into the human condition.

> Morality then, seems to be concerned with three things. Firstly, with fair play and harmony between individuals. Secondly, with what might be called tidying up or harmonizing the things inside each individual. Thirdly, with the general purpose of human life as a whole: what man was made for: what course the whole fleet out to be on: what tune the conductor of the band wants it to play.
>
> You may have noticed that modern people are nearly always thinking about the first thing and forgetting the other two.[2]

Outrage happens when you or I decide that our opinion on how things should be matters most. And when we don't get our way, like a kid in the grocery store who can't have any candy, we throw a temper tantrum. The antidote to outrage is not silencing ourselves, but listening to others.

Thinking again about all the "one anothers" in the Bible, I have a growing awareness of the importance of listening. How can I say I love someone if I am unwilling to listen? Or honor someone? Or serve someone? Or encourage someone? And I'm in good company because many of the different writers in the Bible talk about the value of listening.

- James says, "Everyone should be quick to listen, slow to speak and slow to become angry . . ."[1]
- Solomon tells us to "Listen to advice and accept discipline, and at the end you will be counted among the wise."[2]
- Jesus tells us to "Consider carefully what you hear," and "With the measure you use, it will be measured to you, and even more."[3]

And for our part in the conversation, the other side of listening,

- Paul says, "Do not let any unwholesome talk come out of your mouths, but only what is helpful for building others up according to their needs, that it may benefit those who listen."[4]
- Peter tells us to be like Jesus: "But just as he who called you is holy, so be holy in all you do."[5]
- Paul encourages us, saying, "Don't let anyone look down on you because you are young, but set an example for the believers in speech, in conduct, in love, in faith and in purity."[6]

---

1. James 1:19.
2. Proverbs 19:20.
3. Mark 4:24.
4. Ephesians 4:29.
5. 1 Peter 1:15.
6. 1 Timothy 4:12.

I admit, this is hard to do. We live in a moment that rewards reaction over reflection. Algorithms amplify the most extreme voices because extremity generates attention. Calm explanations do not trend. Nuanced arguments do not go viral. Outrage is efficient. It compresses complex issues into emotionally charged binaries and demands immediate allegiance. But efficiency is not the same as effectiveness. Outrage can mobilize quickly, but it cannot sustain anything.

Social media's role in political expression is double-edged: while platforms can mobilize and inform, they can also facilitate radicalization and the formation of echo chambers. Research on online political communication shows that as traditional social platforms age, usage becomes more fragmented and polarized, with the most active political users often the most ideologically extreme.[3] This fragmentation contributes to environments where outrage thrives, and nuance is lost, and extremist groups exploit these dynamics to spread messaging and recruit and indoctrinate followers, particularly among youth. These structural changes in how Americans consume and share political content have real consequences for civic dialogue, elevating intensity at the expense of listening and reasoned exchange.

One of the most striking challenges to comfortable silence didn't even come from a preacher—it came from outspoken atheist Penn Jillette, who once asked, "How much do you have to hate somebody to believe everlasting life is possible and not tell them that?"[4] Think about that. Even someone who doesn't share the faith understood the basic moral logic: If you really believe something matters eternally, staying quiet isn't kindness. It's neglect. That hits at the heart of where we are as a culture. We've trained people to think conviction is offensive and silence is polite, but real love has never worked that way. Love warns. Love speaks. Love risks awkward conversations because it cares more about people than about comfort. If we want to rebuild a country where truth can actually be discussed instead of shouted down, it starts with recovering that kind of courage—the willingness to speak honestly, not to win arguments, but because we believe people matter too much to leave in the dark.

We need to get back to in-person, face-to-face conversations. Ideally, we need to debate the world we live in while sipping lemonade on our front porches, in coffee shops, at the dinner table, anyplace where we have the time and can make the commitment to care enough to listen, learn, discuss, and debate, and then have a piece of pie. Because, as Mark Twain said, "All that I care to know is that a man is a human being. That's enough for me; he can't be any worse."[8]

How Did We Move from Listening to Shouting?

The call to listen first, then be outspoken but not outrageous, is not a call to soften the truth. It is a call to sharpen it. Outrage blurs distinctions. It collapses complexity. It treats people as symbols rather than souls. Grace, as communicated by the writers of the Bible, does the opposite. It clarifies. It distinguishes. It allows truth to land without unnecessary obstruction.

When people learn how to speak clearly and listen carefully, they become harder to control. They can recognize weak arguments. They can resist emotional manipulation. They can distinguish between conviction and theatrics. That is why every system that depends on control seeks to undermine conversation. It replaces dialogue with directives and persuasion with pressure.

> ***The loss of conversation is not just a cultural inconvenience. It is a strategic vulnerability.***

The loss of conversation is not just a cultural inconvenience. It is a strategic vulnerability. A nation that cannot talk through its differences will eventually try to legislate them away. A society that cannot persuade will eventually punish. And a generation that cannot converse will inherit a politics defined by force rather than reason.

That is not inevitable. But it is the direction we are heading in if we continue to confuse noise with communication and volume with courage.

Conversation is not weakness. It is warfare of a different kind. It is the slow, disciplined work of shaping hearts and minds rather than overpowering them. It requires confidence in truth and respect for human dignity. And it is the only path forward that does not end in tyranny. Conversation is a responsibility that comes with living in a free society, and for believers, it is a calling that comes with bearing the image of God. Words are not incidental to who we are. They are one of the primary ways we exercise stewardship over the world around us. What we say, how we say it, and whether we say it at all shape the moral and cultural terrain long before policies ever do.

In 2009, there was a public outcry following an incident in which Henry Louis Gates Jr., a Harvard University professor, was arrested at his home by local police responding to a 911 call reporting a possible break-in at the address. Because the arresting officer, Sergeant James Crowley, was white, and Gates, the homeowner, was black, there were cries of racism. President Barack Obama, who initially demeaned the actions of the police department, decided to invite Gates and Crowley, both prominent men in their community, to the White House to have a nice, cold beer. The purpose? Presumably, to discuss the incident, race in America, community policing in America, and whatever else President Obama wanted to discuss. It should have been amazing. It could have been an example of meaningful conversation about moments that matter. It might have been three men sipping a cold one while talking, and laughing, and arguing, and learning. There might have been agreeable handshakes and bro-hugs. But, as *Time* so appropriately captured,

> The "beer summit" arranged between Obama, Crowley and Gates was refreshingly down to earth and could have been a publicity coup except for one thing: the media were invited. The three men (plus Joe Biden) sat around a strategically placed table, each drinking his favorite brew, as the press corps watched from across the White House lawn. Instead of a laid-back meeting of minds, the meeting came off looking like a publicity stunt. And what was Biden doing there anyway?[6]

In a world of headlines, posts, videos, and clips, we have lost the art of conversing. We've forgotten (or have never learned) how to have meaningful conversations, go to the gym, spend a day at the beach, ask a question at a community meeting, confront a bully, or mediate a relationship without having a camera rolling just in case something "post-worthy" happens. And we all know, even subconsciously, that there is always a camera rolling, and we are becoming more and more afraid to speak our minds.

In the real world, when having a conversation with a real person, you can't log off. You can't unfollow your neighbor whose sign you disagree with. You can't unfollow the co-worker who dyes her hair blue. You can't block the Bible study guy who dyes his hair orange. This tension, of having to live near people and work with people we disagree with, disciplines speech in ways no platform ever can. Words carry weight because they are tethered to a relationship. Disagreement has consequences, not just reactions. This environment produces a particular kind of citizen, the ones for whom our Founders debated and argued when crafting the Declaration of Independence and the Constitution of the United States. They listened to each other's ideas, surely blew up at each other more than once, and sat back down, perhaps still a little heated, and worked toward their shared goal of serving "We the People." They had to fight to trust each other, because they were all they had.

We cannot rebuild trust through screens alone. Nations heal when people return to places where words have consequences and faces can't be muted. Social media rewards wit, not wisdom. The art of conversation forces patience, and patience is where persuasion lives. Talking and laughing and arguing and learning train people to debate without annihilating and to persuade without posturing. It is possible to listen without surrendering conviction.

Civil discourse and the whole idea of making America talk again is not being polite for the sake of politeness. It is demonstrating restraint for the sake of continuity. It is knowing that you are not speaking *at* an audience; you are conversing with a person, who might just be your neighbor.

A nation doesn't heal through hashtags. It heals when neighbors stop treating each other like enemies and start talking like human beings again, face to face, without a script.

Unfortunately, there are a lot of people who view me as their enemy because I offer my political opinions daily. And we like to create rivalries out of differences, big and small. I didn't understand this when I was younger, but I do now.

I never knew how many enemies one could make until it was time to pick a college. I grew up in the college football capital of the world, Tuscaloosa, Alabama. My favorite thing about Tuscaloosa is that my entire extended family, on both sides, are there. I'm very grateful to have grown up down the road from my grandparents and cousins, and to have had my family grow so close from such an early age. And it wasn't just family that made Tuscaloosa my home. I've bled crimson since birth, and I didn't miss a Bama game at Bryant-Denny Stadium, and I always stayed until the end to sing "Dixieland Delights" with my friends. So, when it came time to decide on where I'd spend my next four years after high school, imagine everybody's shock when I said I was going to apply to Auburn.

I love the athletics and being part of the Roll Tide nation, but I wasn't necessarily attracted to the intense party culture of the campus. But, if you have a pulse, you're probably aware to some degree of the Alabama-Auburn rivalry. It's bigger than football. I vividly remember in kindergarten when our teachers made sure we never put orange and blue crayons together. It was a cardinal sin to make a drawing with Auburn's colors. I even had friends who avoided Auburn on the way to the beach just to say they've never set foot in "that town." Well, "that town" is where I wrote this book during my first semester at that "orange and blue" university.

On my first college tour a few years back, I got invited to speak to the Auburn College Republicans. I was shocked to find that this place I was raised to believe was as close to hell on Earth as it gets . . . was actually beautiful. The campus, the people, the churches. Every category I used to decide on a college was exceeded at Auburn. I got talked into staying the night after my speech and going to a football game the next day. As I was walking through tailgates on campus, I turned to my friend and asked if it was family weekend or something. He looked confused and told me this is just a normal weekend at Auburn: Families with babies and teens running around, throwing corn hole, and watching College GameDay. I've been to over thirty colleges at this point. Never have I found one that has the feel and community that Auburn does. This has taught me to have the courage to speak with people I have been told are my enemies, because they probably are not.

And yes, there are still people who swear at me from across the lawn as I'm walking to and from classes. I have no idea if they disagree with me on the Bible, social issues, global politics, or what. They just curse and keep walking. I have to try to not look over my shoulder.

This is why the breakdown of conversation is not just frustrating, but dangerous. When people lose confidence in their ability to speak and be heard, they stop participating in the public square altogether. They avoid talking to the person holding up a sign on the street. They don't express their opinion to their group of smart-sounding friends because they might be mocked for saying something awkwardly. They don't push back on a new policy being dictated by HR for fear of being fired. They don't ask hard questions of school committee members in an opening meeting out of fear of being canceled. They retreat into private spaces where their views go unchallenged and unrefined. Over time, those private convictions harden into resentments, and resentments do not stay private forever. They surface in uglier, less controlled ways. And with Liberals and a lot of Gen Z, these convictions get screamed into places where no one is listening.

This is especially important in a culture addicted to performance. Outrage is performative by nature. It signals allegiance. It draws applause. It creates an us-versus-them dynamic that feels powerful in the moment. But it also short-circuits persuasion. People who feel attacked do not reconsider their beliefs. They entrench them. Grace creates space. Not space for lies, but space for listening.

Grace is not weakness. It's controlled power, and nothing threatens bullies more than someone they can't provoke into stupidity.

> ***Grace is not weakness. It's controlled power, and nothing threatens bullies more than someone they can't provoke into stupidity.***

Do not be afraid. Do not be frightened. Revere Jesus. Be prepared to give an answer. Give the reason you have hope. Do this with gentleness and respect. Keep a clear conscience. Don't speak maliciously. Don't slander anyone. This is how we make the conversation more civil. If we listen more, have more restraint, and speak the truth in love, the screaming just might get quieter.

A Plea for Passion Without Outrage

Too many people believe that if they are not offending someone, they are not doing enough. Others believe that if they offend the wrong people, they have failed. Both misunderstand the point. The goal is not to offend or to appease. The goal is to communicate truth in a way that can actually be received.

Outrage removes the burden of persuasion. It allows people to express (perform) their convictions in public by marching and protesting and shouting out slogans without doing the work of explaining their ideas, hurts, and wants. It replaces reasoned debate and argument with accusation and substitutes volume for evidence. In doing so, it erodes trust.

People become skeptical not just of the tone, but of the substance behind it.

This chapter is not a rebuke of passion. Passion matters. Conviction matters. Fire matters. But fire without control burns indiscriminately. Grace disciplines passion so that it illuminates rather than destroys. And it starts with listening.

Being outspoken but not outrageous is harder than it sounds. It requires self-control in a culture that rewards impulse. It requires humility in an environment that celebrates dominance. And it requires confidence strong enough to resist the pull of instant validation.

That confidence is rooted in something deeper than reaction. It is rooted in the belief that truth does not need outrage to survive: It needs articulation. And articulation requires discipline.

The outrage economy did not emerge by accident. It is the predictable result of incentives aligned against wisdom. Platforms reward engagement, and outrage is the fastest way to generate it. Anger keeps people scrolling. Fear keeps them clicking. Moral panic keeps them loyal. In that environment, restraint looks inefficient, and patience looks weak. But efficiency is not the same thing as effectiveness, and movements that optimize for attention eventually lose their ability to persuade. Worst of all, the thing we all want most in this life, freedom, doesn't disappear overnight; it erodes while people scroll.

Outrage simplifies. It flattens complex realities into villains and heroes, good people and bad people, enlightened insiders and irredeemable outsiders. That framing feels powerful because it removes ambiguity. You do not have to wrestle with hard questions when everything is already categorized. But simplification comes at a cost. It treats people as problems rather than participants and ideas as threats rather than claims to be examined.

This is why outrage corrodes credibility over time. When everything is framed as a crisis, nothing is. When every disagreement is existential, persuasion becomes impossible. People stop listening not because they disagree, but because they feel manipulated. They sense that emotion is being used to substitute for explanation. Even those who initially agree begin to tune out because constant outrage is exhausting.

The irony is that outrage often masquerades as bravery. It takes nerve to say shocking things. It takes nerve to provoke backlash. But nerve is not the same as courage. Courage is disciplined. It chooses words carefully because it understands their power. Recklessness spends credibility quickly and then wonders why no one trusts it anymore.

Social media doesn't just reflect culture, it trains it. Platforms reward emotional intensity over clarity, certainty over curiosity, outrage over restraint. This shapes how people speak offline, not just online. Over time, users learn that nuanced opinions get buried, while extreme ones get amplified. The result is a generation fluent in reaction but uncomfortable with conversation. When the incentive structure punishes thoughtfulness, silence becomes the rational response. And we can't be silent anymore. We have to start talking again.

Debating Without Demeaning

Nationalized discourse has flattened people into categories. Red or blue. Ally or enemy. Oppressor or victim. This, of course, is at the very center of the plan of the Cultural Marxists—to divide and conquer. In that environment, speech becomes blunt because the audience is abstract. You are no longer responsible for how words land. You are rewarded for how they perform.

When conversation is local, exaggeration collapses quickly. You cannot sustain hysteria when reality is sitting across from you. You cannot demonize someone you know personally without confronting the dissonance. That friction tempers language. It does not eliminate disagreement, but it grounds it.

As politics has nationalized, local responsibility has evaporated. Americans know the names of national influencers but not their school board members. They argue about Supreme Court cases while ignoring city council meetings. This disconnect breeds cynicism because people feel powerless over institutions they no longer participate in. When democracy moves too far away, citizens retreat into commentary instead of contribution. Front-porch politics doesn't just humanize debate; it restores agency. This grounding is what our politics desperately lacks.

Andrew Breitbart famously said that "politics is downstream from culture," but culture itself is downstream from proximity. Screens amplify conflict. Distance breeds caricature. Front porches, neighborhoods, and local institutions force people to confront one another as humans, not avatars. Trust is rebuilt where words have consequences and relationships cannot be muted. We have mistaken reach for influence. A post seen by millions may change nothing. A conversation with a neighbor can change everything.

Influence is not measured by impressions. It is measured by trust. This type of political discussion and debate builds trust because it operates within the community rather than above it.

This does not mean retreating from national issues. It means rehumanizing them. National debates are downstream from local realities. Policies affect people differently depending on where they live, how they work, and what they value.

As I write this, there is a debate in Virginia about government and freedom, taxes and personal responsibility. It is a conversation being had at the state level, but it has implications for all of us. And I want to use this example as a lesson for all of us.

Nick Freitas served as a member of the Virginia House of Delegates. On the matter of debating ideas and how to do it, he previously expressed his concerns (that is, he debated) about the rhetoric of the opposing party. His argument? Instead of debating ideas, he accused Democrats of slandering their Republican colleagues and demeaning America citizens. His speech was thoughtful, powerful, and gracious, since he refused to slander them in return.

> Well, Mr. Speaker, a Democrat has got up and essentially accused us that if we don't want to do what they want to do in order to solve a problem, we're racist or we're mean, or we're stupid, or we're bigoted, or we're incompetent. So it must be any other day of the week, because that's pretty much how this narrative always goes. It's always the party of tolerance that is

immediately ready to accuse us of the worst possible intentions if we disagree.

I thought for a moment we wanted to talk about facts. [Another delegate] got up and she delivered some facts, facts that were relevant with respect to the education of our children. But no, no, no. You're just a racist. It's the same old grift in a different day. And we're tired of it because I don't know anybody on this side of the aisle, and I don't think I know anybody on that side of the aisle that doesn't want to do what's best for our children, but we will disagree on what that is. And I can tell you for all the talk on the other side of the aisle, talking about, "We tried to do this," and "We wanted to do this," and "You voted against it, and because you voted against what the Democrats wanted to do, therefore, you don't care."

Listen, I got to tell you, Mr. Speaker, my constituents look at a lot of the things that our Democrat colleagues want to do, and their response is, "Please stop helping," because they don't know if their business or their child or their family or their community can survive yet another tax, regulation, rule, restriction, fee, government program, government spending. Because I guarantee this much, Mr. Speaker, when it comes to the Democrat side of the aisle, the solution is always the same: Give politicians and bureaucracies more power at the expense of individual liberty, individual freedom, property rights, you name it. We sit here, and we wonder why we have problems in systems which are increasingly under the control of politicians and

> bureaucrats. I don't know about you, Mr. Speaker, but I don't look at many of the challenges that I face in my life and think to myself, you know, what would make this better? Giving politicians more money and power. And yet that seems to be the exclusive approach coming from our friends on the other side of the aisle. And if you don't accept that, if you don't accept a solution that gives them more power, you must be a bad person.
>
> Mr. Speaker, I don't care what they call me anymore. I just don't. Once upon a time, I might have, a little bit, but I don't anymore. Because I see it for what it is. It's not just ideology and political manipulation. Sometimes it's just downright dishonesty. Because, let's face it, we do try to do our best to actually get along around here from time to time. But then, as soon as we're on this floor, all of a sudden, nope, "You don't do what we want, you're a racist, sexist bigoted, suffering from some sort of phobia, or whatever else it is."[7]

I have learned the most influential voices are often the calmest ones in the room. They do not rush to respond. They do not amplify every provocation. They choose their moments. And when they speak, people listen because they know the words were not thrown away casually.

Freitas spoke with conviction and respect. He told the truth and was gracious in doing so. He did not scream or call anyone names. He listened to the other side, discerned the differences between his opinions and theirs, took to the mic, and joined the discussion. Then sat down and listened some more. That is what discourse looks like. And I believe we have a moral obligation to one another to speak the truth, in love, no matter the cost.

Had he said all these things on a social media platform, where he could not see the beautiful faces of those who were calling him and his fellow Republicans names, he might have been snarkier. He might have had less restraint. But here, on the floor of the House of Delegates in Virginia, he was having an in-person conversation with real people. He was talking with them, not at them. He listened before he spoke. He addressed the leadership with respect. He acknowledged the good in those he disagreed with.

Leadership is revealed not by how loudly someone speaks when the room agrees, but by how carefully they speak when the room is divided. In moments of tension, words either widen the fracture or create a bridge strong enough to carry truth across it. The future belongs to those who understand this difference.

Talking to Men about Morality

Instruction is everywhere, but leadership is rare. In particular, young men today are drowning in voices, influencers, commentators, podcasters, and algorithms, yet starving for fathers. We have plenty of people willing to correct behavior, moderate tone, and police language, but very few who are willing to take responsibility for shaping souls. Guardians enforce rules; fathers form men. Guardians keep order; fathers build courage. And when a generation grows up surrounded by guardians but absent of fathers, it learns how to comply, but never how to discern truth, take risks, be courageous, or speak up.

Just look at the headlines:

- "Moral Development and the Phenomenon of Absent Fathers"—American Psychological Association
- "Psychological Effects of Growing Up Without a Father"—Fatherless Boys Foundation
- "Fatherlessness Is One of the True Causes of Crime"—Fox News
- "The Rise of Father Absence and Its Attendant Social Ills"—Quillette

That vacuum has consequences far beyond the home. It gets filled by algorithms, porn, rage politics, counterfeit masculinity, and online figures who promise purpose without responsibility. It shows up in churches, in young men hesitant to step forward, and in a culture where silence feels safer than conviction. When there are no fathers to model strength with humility, truth with love, and courage with sacrifice, young men learn to outsource their moral compass. They wait to be told what's acceptable. They hesitate to speak because no one ever taught them how to stand. Paul didn't just teach the gospel; he embodied it. He called people upward, not because it was comfortable, but because it was necessary. And that kind of leadership is precisely what is missing today.

We talk endlessly about the crisis of masculinity, the collapse of courage, and the silence of young men in the public square, but we rarely trace it back to its root. (And again, this problem is not unique to boys and young men, but to girls and young women, as well.) A generation raised without fathers, spiritual or otherwise, does not naturally rise to confront evil, challenge lies, or speak truth under pressure. It looks for permission. It waits for safety. It defaults to quiet. But the gospel does not produce passive men. It produces sons who grow into fathers and men who speak because they were first spoken to, who stand because someone once stood for them, who answer God's call because someone modeled what obedience looks like when it costs something. Until we recover that kind of fatherhood in homes, churches, and the public square, we should not be surprised when young men stay silent in moments that demand courage.

Young men, let me talk to you plainly, not as a pundit, not as a speaker behind a podium, but as someone your age who sees the vacuum we're living in every single day. We are a generation drowning in opinions but starving for leadership, surrounded by influencers but desperate for men of substance. Too many of us have grown up without models of bold, faithful, grounded Christian manhood to imitate. (That is why so many of us were drawn to conversations with Charlie Kirk: He understood us and met us in the middle of our mess.) We were handed screens instead of standards, affirmation instead of accountability, comfort instead of calling. And the result is a crisis not just of culture, but of courage. Scripture never promises leadership will be easy or applauded, only that it is required. God does not ask young men to wait until they feel ready, healed, confident, or complete before they lead. He asks them to obey. Somewhere along the way, we were told that passivity is humility and conviction is arrogance. That lie has hollowed out churches, families, and communities.

Masculinity has been caricatured as toxic, faith has been privatized into something polite and quiet, and responsibility has been delayed indefinitely. But the world does not need more passive Christian men (and women) who outsource leadership to politics, pastors, or personalities. It needs men willing to stand, speak, protect, build, and sacrifice—men who understand that strength is not domination but responsibility, courage is not noise but consistency, and leadership begins long before anyone is watching. (And once again, I am not excluding young women from the conversation, and in prior generations women would have known that, but I feel called to talk to guys my age directly, so I am.)

This is a call to be faithful. To show up when it would be easier to disappear. To speak when silence would be safer. To lead in your dorm, your church, your workplace, your family, and your friend group long before you are ever handed a title. If our generation is going to change course, it will not be because of another viral moment or a political savior; it will be because young men decide to stop waiting for permission to become the leaders God already called them to be.

CHAPTER 9

Becoming the Kind of Person People Can Talk To

When our children turn the pages of our lives, I hope they'll see that we had a vision to pass forward a nation as nearly perfect as we could, where there's decency, tolerance, generosity, honesty, courage, common sense, fairness, and piety.[1]

—Ronald Reagan

Most people think conversations that change your life arrive with drama, spotlights, speeches, or perfectly timed music swelling in the background. In reality, they usually show up quietly, right in the middle of ordinary life. For me, it happened in a school lunchroom.

I was standing in line with friends, trays in hand, talking about nothing particularly important, weekend plans, homework, whatever high school kids talk about when they're trying to act like life isn't moving faster than they can process. My phone buzzed in my pocket: *Unknown number*. I almost ignored it. Nine times out of ten, it was either a reporter, a prank call, or someone who got my number through a group chat and shouldn't have had it.

I answered anyway, half-distracted, and said a dry, unenthusiastic, "Yes, hello."

On the other end was a familiar voice, a friend of mine calling from her brand-new government phone, now working in the West Wing. She didn't waste time with small talk.

"Are you free tomorrow?"

I laughed. "If you write me a school excuse."

She told me the reason for the call. The president of the United States, the forty-fifth and now forty-seventh, was coming to my hometown to deliver the University of Alabama commencement address. There would be a short window backstage. Would I like a few minutes to catch up?

I remember responding without missing a beat: "Do Kamala [Harris] and Nancy [Pelosi] drink Grey Goose on days that end in 'y'? Of course, I'll be there."

Who wouldn't say yes?

I went back to class that day, knowing something huge was coming but still trying to act normal.

The next afternoon, once my classes ended for the day, I went home, changed into a suit, headed to campus, and walked into a world that felt completely different from the one I had been sitting in just hours earlier.

Backstage at Coleman Coliseum doesn't feel glamorous. It feels tight. Controlled. Efficient. You don't linger. You don't wander. You wait. And as I stood in line, it hit me how out of place I looked. Everyone ahead of me seemed to belong to another universe entirely, people with last names I recognized from buildings I'd driven past my whole life, people whose net worth was longer than my phone number. Donors. Power brokers. Advisors. Executives. I was just a kid who had started a podcast in fourth grade and refused to shut up. Then my name was called.

The president turned his head. "Brilyn Hollyhand."

And just like that, I was the very last person to meet with President Donald J. Trump before he was escorted onstage to address fifteen thousand graduates.

"I saw you on Fox this morning," he said. "You killed it."

Then he turned to White House Press Secretary Karoline Leavitt and repeated it, louder this time. "This kid killed it. He killed it."

We talked about the question that has defined my work for years: How do you make sure Gen Z isn't a one-cycle phenomenon? How do you keep young voters engaged in 2026, 2028, and beyond?

I told him he had a secret weapon.

He raised an eyebrow. "What's that?"

I said, "This brand-new concept in politics called 'actually doing what we campaigned on and keeping our promises to voters.' I know that's revolutionary, but it's why Gen Z is moving to the right, by the day."

He laughed, but he listened.

Then he said something I'll never forget: "Gen Z has the potential to be the greatest generation, if you work hard and put your minds to it."

He leaned in and asked how big the crowd was.

"Fifteen thousand students," I told him.

He smiled.

Then, in true Trump fashion, he asked the most unexpected question of all: "Are they playing any good music?"

I told him I'd been stuck in the basement waiting, but had heard "YMCA" earlier.

His face lit up. "That's my favorite song," he said, laughing and doing the dance.

And just like that, the greatest coach in all of college sports, Nick Saban, appeared at the doorway to walk the president on stage. That was my cue.

A few minutes later, the commander in chief, in his fifth month back in office, shared these words of wisdom to a crowd full of students:

> If you're here today and think that you're too young to do something great, let me tell you that you are wrong. You're not too young. You can have great success at a very young age. You're all very young. In America, with drive and ambition, young people can do anything. I was 28 when I took my first big gamble to develop a hotel in Midtown Manhattan, the Grand Hyatt. And it worked out incredibly well. But I was very young at the time. I was like a very young person in sort of an old person business. Steve Jobs was 21

> when he founded Apple. Walt Disney was 21 when he founded Disney.[2]

That meeting backstage wasn't about status or access. It was a reminder of why this book exists in the first place. Politics isn't preserved by slogans or soundbites; it's preserved by honest conversations between leaders and citizens, between generations, between a kid and the president.

And if we stop talking, really talking, we don't just lose elections; we lose the country.

Just in the first few weeks of 2026, looking back at the Winter Olympic protests, the NFL halftime-show debates, and the flag-burning demonstrations that filled the news cycle, none of it actually surprised me. By the time those moments exploded publicly, the groundwork had already been laid in classrooms and cultural messaging for years.

I'd seen it firsthand—sitting in lecture halls where America was framed more as a problem than a promise, where we dissected every national failure but rarely studied the miracle of self-government or the principles that drew millions here in the first place.

On campus, I heard classmates say they were ashamed to be American, not because they had deeply wrestled with history, but because that posture felt socially safe. Pride was risky. Guilt was rewarded. So when athletes criticized the country they represented, entertainers used national stages to signal that the "old America" was over, or protesters burned flags while claiming moral authority, it didn't feel like a sudden shift. It felt like the natural result of what my generation had been taught to believe.

The real issue wasn't the protests themselves—it was the pipeline behind them. If you teach a generation that America is primarily oppressive, don't be shocked when they start acting like they're representing something shameful. A nation can survive honest criticism, but it cannot survive when its own children are embarrassed by it. Gratitude and accountability were never supposed to compete; both are part of the full story. But somewhere along the way, we stopped telling that full story and started training young Americans to swap gratitude for guilt. And when that happens, the cultural explosions we saw weren't the beginning of the problem—they were the visible symptom of a deeper lesson plan already in motion.

Here Am I. Send Me.

Eventually, every believer meets the question that exposes whether faith is real or just familiar: "Whom shall I send?" Most people admire Isaiah's answer, "Here am I. Send me!" Far fewer people are willing to live it.

Isaiah's answer did not come from confidence. It came from clarity. He did not volunteer because the mission sounded safe, popular, or winnable. In fact, if you keep reading, God immediately tells him the truth: the people will not listen, the message will be rejected, the work will be confusing, heavy, and lonely. Isaiah says yes anyway.

That is what makes the response so powerful.

If I could sit across from the kid I used to be, the one with the cheap mic and the small audience, I wouldn't tell him it gets easier. I'd tell him it gets clearer. That fear doesn't vanish, but purpose sharpens. That obedience often looks unimpressive in the moment. And God rarely explains the full cost before asking for a yes.

But I'd also tell him this: Every time you choose truth over comfort, you'll sleep better at night, even when the world is loud.

Mentors for the Next Generation

Before Charlie was killed, he told me to read *The Age of Entitlement* by Christopher Caldwell. In the 1960s, the assassination of President John F. Kennedy shocked the nation, shattering our sense of safety. The ongoing tension of race relations was at a boiling point as segregation was being dismantled. And the politics of the Vietnam War undermined our sense of civic duty. That sure does sound a lot like today, doesn't it? After the assassination attempts on Donald Trump and the assassination of Charlie Kirk, we are all on edge. Ongoing revelations and rhetoric about illegal immigration and ICE, election integrity, and insider trading have infuriated most of us. And the demise of education in our country has undermined our sense of civic duty. For me, and for many of you, Charlie stood and spoke as a mentor for our generation. We owe him a great debt.

With the grief of Charlie's murder still fresh, I spent some time in October 2025 with another mentor, Brandon Tatum. During our podcast interview, we talked about Charlie, politics, hustle, student movements, faith, and more. Most significantly, we talked about the influence of Gen Z and how the conservative movement—no, the American Experiment—needs young people right now. We also talked about my frustration that so many people in our movement love to scream that they want to see the next generation get off the sidelines and into the fight, but when a young person is sacrificing his childhood and college education to get off the sidelines and into the fight, then they are the first person they want to attack. I'd expect that criticism from the Left. I didn't expect that from my peers.

In that conversation, Brandon made a great point that we all need to embrace as we keep going:

> Why be jealous or hate on somebody? And if you think they have imperfections, how about you step out of your comfort zone and help the person become what you need them to be? Because Charlie is no longer here. And it's going to take a lot of young people. . . . We need every young person, whether you're seasoned or not, or whether you feel comfortable or not, everybody needs to get out and do something. You got to do something. I love the fact that you're operating in God's calling on your life to just get out and do something.[3]

We need more faith in politics. We need more Jesus on college campuses. We need more truth in media boardrooms. We need more grace in our conversations. We need more mentors guiding younger generations. And we need more faithful, conservative-minded people to start talking.

If you have a lot of experience and wisdom to share with younger generations, please, do so. If you are young and have someone in your life who you can learn from and trust to challenge what you have been taught to believe, please, do so. Of course, we need more peer-to-peer conversations, but we also need more generation-to-generation conversations. And given the number of people I've talked to and listened to in the last two years, I promise you, it is worth it.

The Future of America

For all the cynicism surrounding politics today, and regardless of what happened with Mamdani in New York City,[4] the most hopeful data point is this: young Americans still believe in the idea of democracy, even when they're frustrated with its execution. Surveys show that the younger members of Gen Z overwhelmingly reject authoritarianism, value freedom, and want institutions that live up to their promises.[5] That combination of skepticism paired with conviction is not a weakness, it's a strength waiting to be activated.

This generation is also massive. Millions of new young voters entered the electorate leading into 2024, making Gen Z one of the largest and most influential generations in American history.[6] That's not a future statistic. That's now. Which means the decisions made in living rooms, dorm rooms, churches, and classrooms today will echo for decades.

And here's the most important part: Engagement doesn't just shape elections. It shapes people. Research consistently shows that young adults who vote, volunteer, and participate in civic life develop stronger communities, deeper purpose, and greater resilience. In other words, stepping into responsibility doesn't just change the country; it changes you.

That's the invitation of this chapter. Not to chase power. Not to win arguments. But to become the kind of person that people want to talk to, and answer the call when it comes. To look at the moment you were born into, messy, loud, divided, and full of need, and walk into it. I know what you're thinking. This is scary. Why would I do this? I'm not here to gaslight you. It's as scary as it gets. But that's why you should do it.

In my first semester in college, I went on a ten-stop campus tour.[7] Every stop came with warnings. Every stop came with threats. Every stop came with more metal detectors, drones, and dogs. And at one campus, posters announcing the event, ones that depicted a photo of me, were torn in half, leaving half of my brutalized picture for me to see.

I remember asking God, "Why me? Why now? Why this?" I remember thinking how easy it would be to put the mic down and go back to being a normal student. Go to class. Do homework. Binge-watch Netflix with friends. Live quietly. Safely.

Benjamin Franklin's warning about "a republic, if you can keep it," was never about parchment or procedure. It was about people. A republic survives only as long as ordinary citizens accept extraordinary responsibility. Institutions cannot substitute for courage. And the future of America needs more courage. And it needs you.

Throughout the Bible, God's people are called not to withdraw from the world, but to engage it with clarity and courage. We are to be a part of our cities and obey the law.

Now, you may argue there is something out there you have heard, a slogan of sorts, something about the "separation of church and state." I'd be shocked if you had not heard that. But this idea, or the last one hundred years of lying about it, is a perversion of reality. This idea, when expressed by the leaders of the founding era, was always about protecting citizens' religious freedom from government abuses of power. It was never about compelling faith to be a private matter. Never. How can you argue with the fruit of sincere, abiding, Christian faith? Remember, "the fruit of the Spirit is love, joy, peace, patience, kindness, goodness, faithfulness, gentleness and self-control." Of this, even the Bible says, "against such things there is no law."[1] Who in their right mind would say we don't want more of these things in our school board meetings, Sunday morning shows, courtrooms, boardrooms, and public discourse as a whole? Who would outlaw such things? Not me. And I hope, not you. Because, as Mark Twain said, "Kindness is a language which the deaf can hear and the blind can read."[8]

As you think about the future of America and your role in it, what does that look like? How can you become more comfortable with listening than talking? Better at defending your ideas rather than "owning" someone in an argument? Well, it does not start with taking more public speaking classes or simply reading more books (though those definitely help!). It starts with understanding why the Fruit of the Spirit matters at all.

When Do's and Don'ts Change the Discussion

The modern temptation is to treat conversation as optional, something we can outsource to professionals or avoid altogether. We tell ourselves that posting is enough, or voting is enough, or staying quiet is a form of humility. But humility does not mean hiding what you believe. It means holding

1. Galatians 5:22–23, ESV.

it with confidence rather than arrogance. It means speaking truth without contempt and listening without surrender. It means making eye contact, having a firm handshake, and learning from the wisdom of dads from old TV shows. But most importantly, it means being the kind of person who cares about people more than themselves and having the conviction and courage to tell the truth.

If you want to become the kind of person who loves others naturally, honors friends and family, the kind of person who people want to laugh with, love, work with, and more, you need to know there are things that are good for you to do, and things that are not. You can't just show up and demand that people listen; you have to ask for permission to talk and prove that you can be a safe person to debate ideas and share feelings with. You need to become more like Jesus and less like those who are conceited and provoke and envy others.

That balance is difficult, but it is not impossible. First and foremost, it requires faith. Then it requires practice. It requires failure. It requires the willingness to be awkward, misunderstood, and occasionally wrong. It demands that we care more about conversations than clicks and likes. It involves doing some things that might get you booed by people who are quick to judge you for your faith. It means ignoring the threats of cancel culture and putting away your fear in pursuit of something better. And it looks a whole lot like having the courage to disagree with those who think "sexual immorality, impurity and debauchery; idolatry and witchcraft; hatred, discord, jealousy, fits of rage, selfish ambition, dissensions, factions and envy; drunkenness, orgies, and the like" are good. And if you are having a hard time with this list of sinful behavior listed in the Bible, you are not alone. Mark Twain said of the Bible, "Most people are bothered by those passages of Scripture they do not understand, but the passages that bother me are those I do understand."[9]

The choice before us is not between conversation and conflict. It is between conversation now and conflict later. Disagreement is inevitable. The question is whether we will handle it with words or with weapons, with persuasion or with pressure. A society that cannot tolerate disagreement cannot remain free, no matter how noble its intentions.

The TV show *Landman* lit a firestorm in 2025 when it dared to portray what is likely a common conversation on a college campus. In the season two finale, Ainsley Norris, a not-too-bright but savvy girl who has a mom who treats her like a bestie and a dad who doesn't know what to do about her wild side, meets her college roommate, Paigyn, from Minneapolis. Based on Paigyn's demeanor, attire, and haircut, it is difficult to say if this person is supposed to be a young woman or a young man who somehow ends up with a female roommate.

The conversation starts simply with curiosities about on-campus athletics and majors before Paigyn corrects Ainsley for wrongly asking if the name is "like the godless religion," telling her it is Latin. And after Paigyn introduces a pet ferret to Ainsley, an animal that she has no idea about, Ainsley asks about an air freshener, at which point Paigyn takes over the conversation, driving home different approaches to gracious behavior and conversations.

We quickly learn that air fresheners are "toxic airborne petrochemicals" before Paigyn asks Ainsley her pronouns and announces that Paigyn's pronouns are they/them. Ainsley explains she has never understood the "hoopla of pronouns" or the reason for using plural pronouns, and explains the reasonable expectation that a person should never be referred to in the third person while in the same room anyway.

We then learn that the word *penetrate* "insinuates the patriarchal power of the phallus," and Paigyn forbids the use of it, even when talking about how well skincare products work. Furthermore, Ainsley should not eat meat in the room because Paigyn is a vegan and does not want any animal products of any kind in the room, including Ainsley's cowhide boots, and that Paigyn meditates at noon and does not like music to be played in the room at any time. And then there is the conversation ender: "This is my safe space, and I need my environment crafted to support my mental health."[10]

Now, Ainsley is no role model for young women anywhere. But throughout the conversation, she is kind, patient, gentle, and self-controlled. It is hard to watch her joy-filled expectations of her first day of school crushed by a single conversation and replaced with tears.

A conversation that begins with listening and not spouting a list of demands can heal the confusion. It has the power to mend relationships and bring peace where there is disagreement. And we have the power to decide what kind of person we want to be and what type of conversations we want to have. Southern hospitality may be a lost art in most of the country, but good and honoring conversations do not have to be.

Recovering the lost art of conversation will not be easy. It requires unlearning habits that have been rewarded for years. It requires resisting the incentives that push us toward outrage and withdrawal. It requires courage to speak when silence feels safer and discipline to listen when anger feels justified. But the alternative is far worse.

Conversation is how trust is rebuilt. It is how misunderstandings are corrected. It is how truth spreads without coercion. And it is how a divided people finds common ground without pretending differences do not exist.

The lost art of conversation must be recovered—not because it makes us feel better, but because without it, we are incapable of defending anything worth keeping.

So, speak clearly. Listen carefully. Refuse to confuse noise with courage or silence with wisdom. Treat conversation not as a risk to be managed, but as a responsibility to be embraced. And become the person your friends, family, coworkers, and neighbors want to talk to because a nation that cannot talk honestly to itself will eventually be spoken for by someone else.

Want to know how to get started? Here are a couple of books that will give you some pointers. (Yes, they are on my reading list, too!)

- *How to Win Friends and Influence People: The Only Book You Need to Lead You to Success* by Dale Carnegie
- *17 Essential Qualities of a Team Player: Becoming the Kind of Person Every Team Wants* by John C. Maxwell

- *The 7 Habits of Highly Effective People: Powerful Lessons in Personal Change* by Stephen R. Covey
- *Dare to Lead: Brave Work. Tough Conversations. Whole Hearts.* by Brené Brown
- *Toxic Empathy: How Progressives Exploit Christian Compassion* by Allie Beth Stuckey

Conclusion
Saving America at the Dinner Table

And let me offer lesson number one about America: All great change in America begins at the dinner table.[1]
—Ronald Reagan

Before America was divided by parties, it was held together by conversations. If we can't disagree at the dinner table without breaking the relationship, we have no business pretending we can hold a republic together.

Long before Americans argued on cable news or posted opinions online, they argued across tables. Wooden ones. Scratched ones. Crowded ones. Dinner tables where voices overlapped, disagreements lingered, and convictions were tested not by strangers, but by people you loved. That was where democracy learned to breathe—not in polished studios or curated feeds, but in homes where disagreement had consequences and relationships forced restraint.

The dinner table is where courage was trained. Conversation is not instinctive. It is practiced. The dinner table taught America how to argue without destroying relationships. When those conversations died, polarization moved in.

President Ronald Reagan understood this when he encouraged people to get back to the dinner table. He was not romanticizing nostalgia. He was diagnosing a truth about human formation. Public convictions are shaped privately. The habits that govern how we disagree in public are learned long before we ever enter the public square. They are learned at home, where you cannot block, mute, or cancel the person across from you. That friction matters. If you can't survive a disagreement with your own family, you're not prepared to steward a republic.

Some of the most clarifying conversations I've had didn't happen on stages or in front of cameras. They happened in high school lunchrooms, college dining halls, and family kitchens. In trucks. On back porches. With people who don't care about clicks or talking points; they care about groceries, kids, faith, and whether America still feels like home.

Those conversations remind me why this matters. Not because politics is everything, but because it touches everything. And when everyday people stop talking honestly, the vacuum is filled by the loudest voices—not the wisest.

The story of the early church, and more specifically the actions and teachings of the first followers of Jesus, is recorded in the Book of Acts in the Bible. In it, we find one of the simplest yet most profound messages we need to hear today. After being arrested for talking about Jesus, the men were free, and they were again talking in public about the teachings of Jesus. When harassed by the political leaders who demanded an explanation, Peter and the other followers of Jesus replied, "We must obey God rather than human beings!"[1]

This historical moment captures the tension every free society must navigate. Obedience to God over men does not eliminate conflict. It clarifies allegiance. The followers of Jesus did not retreat from public life because authority opposed them. They spoke anyway, knowing that obedience carried a cost. But that obedience was not impulsive. It was cultivated through a life of disciplined conversation, reasoning, and community. And I bet it happened while sitting around the campfire toasting some bread and cooking some fish.

America has witnessed the quiet collapse of local institutions that once held civic life together. Rotary clubs, church committees, town halls, and neighborhood associations all declined as national media replaced local relationships. Is this a problem? The good folks at American Enterprise Institute think so:

> This is not just a cultural loss; it is a civic one. The decline of third places contributes to rising loneliness,

1. See Acts 5:17–42.

> weaker social trust, and declining engagement with neighbors. Social capital does not regenerate itself—it is produced in spaces where people encounter one another with regularity and low stakes. When those encounters disappear, people stop learning how to share space with those unlike themselves, and difference begins to feel threatening rather than ordinary. We can talk endlessly about polarization, but a nation without shared physical spaces loses the habits that make democratic life possible.[2]

People became politically informed but socially disconnected. They knew what was happening in Washington, but not who lived next door.

This shift hollowed out trust. When disagreements are mediated through screens instead of shared spaces, empathy disappears. Political opponents stop being neighbors and start being abstractions. Conversation gives way to caricature. Conflict escalates because there is no relational cost to cruelty.

Democracies depend on proximity. When citizens stop encountering one another as humans, the system fractures. The loss of local politics didn't just change how Americans talked; it changed whether they could.

We often assume that cultural collapse begins in legislatures or courtrooms. More often, it begins in living rooms: When families stop talking about hard things, when disagreement is treated as disrespect, when children learn peace is maintained by silence rather than truth, these lessons do not stay at home. They scale.

> ***A generation raised without conversation does not suddenly learn it in adulthood.***

A generation raised without conversation does not suddenly learn it in adulthood. The decline of the dinner table has not been accidental. As schedules fractured and screens replaced presence, conversation became optional. According to a BBC survey conducted in 2025, 51 percent of children surveyed said they used their phones while eating. Approximately 66 percent of kids said they would prefer to watch TV while eating instead of with a parent. And 77 percent of families said that their phones are often at the table during meals.[3] It wasn't like this in the sixties, seventies, or eighties. Or even the nineties. But at some point, meals became rushed or isolated. Families ate separately, distracted, or not at all. With that shift, something essential was lost. Not information, but formation.

At the dinner table, children learn to disagree without dehumanizing others. They learn how to ask questions without assuming malice. They learn conviction does not require volume, and listening does not require surrender. Or they learn the opposite. They learn certain topics are forbidden, harmony depends on avoidance, and truth is dangerous when it disrupts comfort. Those lessons shape citizens.

The dinner table also teaches courage in a way no public forum can. It is easier to argue with strangers than with family. Strangers carry no relational weight. Family does. Speaking honestly at the table risks tension that does not disappear when the conversation ends. You still have to pass the potatoes. You still have to show up next week. That constraint disciplines speech. It also strengthens it.

This is why so many people feel more confident posting opinions than speaking them aloud. Online, disagreement is abstract. At the table, it is embodied. Tone matters. Timing matters. Love matters. The dinner table forces you to consider all three simultaneously. It trains you to speak with conviction and care because the relationship cannot be discarded. That training is indispensable to democracy. Almost as much as obeying God.

Is America a Christian Nation?

When families stop talking about faith, politics, and values, children learn these topics are either irrelevant or too dangerous to engage with. Neither lesson produces courageous citizens. Both produce silence masquerading as maturity.

Rebuilding conversation at the dinner table and everywhere we meet with friends and family is not about nostalgia. It is about infrastructure. Democracy depends on citizens who have practiced disagreement in environments where love limits cruelty and truth demands clarity. That practice does not begin on campus or in Congress. It begins at home, in a country that was built on a religious creed that should matter to us all.

At the memorial for Charlie Kirk, Vice President JD Vance made a comment about talking more about his faith publicly in the two weeks after the assassination than he had during his entire political career combined. His courage, his renewal of faith, is shaping the future of America. At the 2026 America Fest, Vice President Vance explained the idea of American identity to us all:

The only thing that has truly served as an anchor of the United States of America is that we have been, and by the grace of God, we always will be, a Christian nation. Now, I want to be explicit, because, of course, the fake news media will twist everything that I say. I'm not saying you have to be a Christian to be an American. I'm saying something simpler and truer. Christianity is America's creed. The shared moral language from the Revolution to the Civil War and beyond. Across that history, our country's major debates have always centered on how we could best, as a people, please God. That creed motivated our understanding of natural law and rights, our sense of duty to one's neighbor, the conviction that the strong must protect the weak, and the belief in individual conscience. Even our famously American idea of religious liberty is a Christian concept. Because we're all creatures of God, we must respect each individual's pathway to that God.

But over the last 50 years, there has been a singular focus, a war that has been waged on Christians and Christianity in the United States of America. And let me say, of all the wars that Donald Trump has ended, that is the one we're proudest of.

For decades, the Left has labored to push Christianity out of national life. They've kicked it out of the schools, out of the workplace, out of the fundamental parts of the public square. Freedom *of* religion transformed into freedom *from* religion. And in a public square devoid of God, we got a vacuum. And the ideas that filled that void preyed on the very worst of human nature

> rather than uplifting it. They told us not that we were children of God, but children of this or that identity group. They replaced God's beautiful design for the family, that men and women could rely on and turn to one another, with the idea that men could turn into women so long as they bought the right bunch of pills from Big Pharma. They had all the religious fervor of a zealous convert without any of the grace or forgiveness of a true Christian.
>
> Scripture tells us, "By your fruits ye shall know them." And we might ask, "What are the fruits of these people and their principles?" And the answer is a man named Tyler Robinson, who killed my friend. Think about it. He has everything that the far Left want from our young men. He rejected the conservatism and the spirituality, the values of his small-town family. He moved into a small apartment. He became addicted to porn. He became addicted to hate. And he ended up sleeping with somebody who doesn't know whether they're a man or a woman. That is the nightmare scenario. But that is the scenario that the Left has actively advertised they want for American families, and the young men in the audience in particular. That is exactly why we have to fight them, because the fruits of true Christianity are men like Charlie Kirk.[4]

The dinner table is not just a place to eat. It is a training ground. It is where we learn to be polite, say please and thank you, respect our elders, pray for our enemies, and love one another. And Vice President Vance so righteously explained, when dinner-table conversation disappears, it leaves a vacuum, one that will always be filled. In our moment, that something has been outrage culture, algorithmic tribalism, and a generation trained to react rather than reason. Private silence does not produce public peace. It produces public chaos.

Is America a Christian nation? Yes. And I'm tired of being lectured to feel guilty for it. If the fruit of being a Christian nation is having friends, family, coworkers, bosses, strangers, sports rivals, television personalities, standup comedians, and politicians all being more loving, joyful, peaceful, patient, kind, good, faithful, gentle, and self-controlled, why would anyone want to write a law to prevent that?

Restoring America's Families

When families recover conversation, they recover formation. When formation is restored, citizens become capable of disagreement without destruction. And when that capacity spreads, democracy regains its footing.

A generation willing to speak at home will not remain silent in public. That is the thought history keeps confirming, and culture keeps forgetting. The courage required to obey God rather than men does not materialize in moments of national crisis. It is forged in ordinary rooms, around ordinary tables, through conversations that are anything but ordinary.

In 2021, the American College of Pediatricians noted the benefits of the family table, saying, "The custom of regularly eating together as a family is common to most cultures. There are proven benefits to every member when mealtime is a family affair. Families today, however, are less likely to gather at meal times than in the past. Given the protective factors that are conveyed to children and adolescents, pediatricians should encourage parents to make every effort to regularly gather around the 'Family Table' for meals."[5] Their research found that "Over the past three decades, family time at the dinner table and family conversation, in general, has declined by more than 30%," and in their prescription on how to implement the value of the family table, they suggest "during the meal encourage pleasant and respectful conversation."[6]

When children are invited into serious conversation early, they learn that truth is not fragile. They learn that disagreement does not signal danger. They learn that authority can be challenged without being destroyed and conviction can be expressed without cruelty. Those lessons create adults who are steady under pressure, not reactive to it. Steadiness is rare right now because formation has been outsourced.

Many parents assume schools, churches, or media will handle the hard conversations. Others avoid them altogether, hoping children will arrive at adulthood unscathed by controversy. But avoidance is not neutrality. It is instruction. It teaches that silence is safer than truth, and peace depends on pretending. Those lessons do not prepare people for a world that will demand clarity.

The dinner table does not guarantee agreement. It guarantees exposure. Exposure to opposing views. Exposure to consequences. Exposure to the reality that obedience costs something. That exposure is protective. It inoculates against panic when pressure mounts. It teaches that discomfort is not an emergency.

Regularly, after speeches or even on sidewalks, parents complain to me about the failure that is public education today. I know what they are saying. I am living it. But my response to those parents every single time is simple: Educate your kids in the living room before they're indoctrinated in the classroom.

> ***Educate your kids in the living room before they're indoctrinated in the classroom.***

When faith and values are discussed openly at home, children learn belief is not reserved for Christmas and Easter, and it shapes choices. It carries implications. It may require sacrifice. Those realities are easier to accept when they are normalized early rather than introduced abruptly later. Parents can do something that I can only try to do: teach their kids the truth before it is too late. It is not inevitable that every child will grow up saying, as Mark Twain did, "When I was a boy of fourteen, my father was so ignorant I could hardly stand to have the old man around. But when I got to be twenty-one, I was astonished at how much he learned in seven years."[7] And if you wait till they are twenty-three, and out of college, you will have sent them off to college as sons and daughters whom you love, only to have them return as non-binary brats who hate you.

When I finished my college tour registering voters, I remembered a moment from my senior year of high school, registering all of my friends to vote in the lunch room one day. At the time, I was surprised that schools didn't make it a homework assignment to register to vote. (And I'm still shocked that high schools don't require speech and debate classes.) But here I was, a freshman in college, and I could relate to this crazy period of picking a college and saying goodbye to high school. Most of my peers weren't thinking about registering to vote before the midterms, so I wanted to do something about it.

While sharing my concern with a friend who is a state representative about low youth voter turnout in my own home state, she invited me to fix that at the high schools in her district. That conversation sparked my high school voter registration tour during the spring semester.

In the first week, I put a lot of miles on my car driving to seven different high schools to talk to seniors and throw a QR code up onscreen to make it easy for them to register to vote. Most of the students were already eighteen, and their vote counts just as much as those of my classmates at college. And getting to them in high school reduces the likelihood of indoctrination in college. But why is it my job? Why do I have to get high school kids to register to vote? Where are the parents? Where is the family table? I ask these questions, not to demean or berate parents who live in a culture intent on stealing their kids from them, but to challenge us all to do our part. And proximity is directly related to influence. Speaking to all the parents with small kids who might be reading this book, I might only get sixty minutes in a high school to talk to your son or daughter about civics before they go to college. You get eighteen years.

Gen Z Is Making America Talk Again

There is something going on in the youth of America today. And while the outpouring of love and grief and the increase in the purchases of the Bible and church attendance after Charlie's murder point to his remarkable role in shaping the future of America, his life and legacy are not the only good in the world. Faithful pastors are preaching what the Bible says about politics and morality and are calling evil by its name. Honorable parents are running for school boards and starting homeschool groups. Courageous men and women are running for local office. And more and more Christians are overcoming the lie they have been told—that their faith is private. And we are seeing the effects of this righteous behavior in the lives of Gen Z.

At most Q&As I do, one of the first questions is, "Why do you go to college if Charlie said college was a scam?" Well, he was right. It absolutely is a scam. You're giving up at least four years for a piece of paper and taxpayer-funded obedience training. High school counselors today should encourage students that there are other paths than just what's in the pamphlet: trade schools, community colleges, and the workforce. I have friends who skipped school and are plumbers who make more than my friends in accounting, who are still paying off their debt.

There are three reasons I'm at one of those taxpayer-funded obedience training centers:

1. If we wave the white flag and abandon them, there won't be credible opposing voices of reason pushing back against the propaganda being heaped upon naïve students who are being told to "trust the science" and obey their blue-haired professors.
2. I taught myself how to do this business in the fourth grade when I started my podcast, and I've learned

everything else along the way. I had no courses or lectures on surviving the darkest arena in the workforce, that is, politics. So, a political science degree has been super fun in teaching me the fundamentals and giving me context to quote, like specific founding documents, laws, or historical examples to strengthen my debates on TV. (Charlie did this by taking a crazy amount of Hillsdale College courses online over the past few years.)

3. I spent most of my childhood with one foot in the adult world and one foot still on the playground with my friends. I'd do it all again in a heartbeat, but speaking on campuses hasn't resulted in missing movie nights, birthday parties, and camping trips with my buddies. College has allowed me to live with and do life with all my friends while also joining Fox News from the corner of my dorm before and after class.

And my efforts are part of a larger movement of truth that is making a difference. Across eighty-four of the eighty-eight major college campuses, Generation Z shifted eleven points to the right, a double-digit movement in the very demographic we were told was permanently lost, ideologically owned, and culturally sealed off by the Democratic Party.[8] For years, we were lectured that young voters were destined to be progressive by default, conservatism was aging out, and campuses were irreversibly captured by the radical Left. The data obliterated that narrative in one election cycle.

This wasn't driven by a single candidate or a fleeting moment of outrage. It was the cumulative effect of lived reality colliding with ideology. Students who were promised liberation found themselves buried under inflation, priced out of housing, drowning in student debt, and silenced in classrooms that preached "diversity" while punishing dissent. They were told speech was violence, biology was optional, merit was oppressive, and the American story was something to apologize for. Eventually, enough of them looked around and asked a dangerous question: What if the people shouting the loudest don't actually have the answers?

That's why this shift matters. Political realignments don't happen because of slogans; they happen when common sense reasserts itself after being ignored for too long. Gen Z didn't move right because they suddenly became partisan warriors; they moved because reality became impossible to ignore. They rejected chaos disguised as compassion, censorship sold as safety, and radicalism marketed as progress. What happened on those campuses wasn't a fluke. It was the early signal of a generation rediscovering that stability, freedom, and truth still matter, and the radical, woke Left has no monopoly on youth anymore.

The coolest thing I've ever gotten to do came the day after the 2024 Republican National Convention in Milwaukee. I talked the campaign into supporting my out-of-the-box idea to speak at the largest country music festival in the South, appropriately called "Rock the South." Before Eric Church performed that night, I walked onstage, in front of the thirty thousand people spread out across the field, and urged them to use the phones to scan the QR code I put on the Jumbotrons to register to vote. It was only a few days since Donald Trump raised his fist in a similar field in Butler,

Pennsylvania, and before I even finished giving instructions, the entire crowd started chanting "Fight, Fight, Fight."

What I heard in that field wasn't just a chant. It was a reminder. A reminder that beneath the noise, beneath the division, beneath the headlines telling us we're too broken to fix, there is still something alive in this country worth fighting for. Not fighting with fists. Not fighting with hatred. But fighting for the kind of nation where people still believe their voice matters, their vote matters, and their neighbor is worth talking to—even when they disagree.

That moment in the field didn't feel like a campaign event. It felt like a glimpse of what America still can be—ordinary people showing up, standing shoulder to shoulder, and choosing to care about the future. The real fight ahead isn't against each other. It's against the apathy, the silence, and the cynicism that convince us nothing can change. Because once people believe that, the story really does end.

But I don't believe that. I believe the story of this country is still being written by people willing to step up, speak out, and choose conversation over chaos. That's what this book has been about from the first page to the last: not nostalgia for what America used to be, but a challenge for what it still could become if we're willing to rebuild the habits that hold a free society together—courage, faith, responsibility, and the simple willingness to listen before we shout.

The future won't be decided by the loudest voices on social media or the angriest headlines on cable news. It will be decided in conversations, at dinner tables, on campuses, in churches, in town halls, and in moments like that field in

Alabama where thousands of people chose to stand up and engage instead of tune out.

So if you've read this far, the baton and the microphone are in your hands now. The question isn't whether the country needs rebuilding. The question is whether we're willing to do the work, to speak when it's uncomfortable, to listen when it's hard, and to stand firm when it would be easier to stay quiet.

This isn't the end of the story.

It's the part where you decide what happens next.

Acknowledgments

Thank you, God: Before any of my family or team, I want to thank my Lord and Savior not only for the breath in my lungs but for the courage and platform to write this book you're holding. There is no statistical way a fourth grader with a dream and a cheap microphone should have made it. If you don't know Jesus, there's never been a better time to give your life to Him. This book highlighted countless examples of how broken our society is. Don't chase a worldly answer to fill that God-shaped hole in your life. Save the time and pain and surrender today. Give Jesus your all, because He gave His all for you.

Thank you, Mom and Dad: I don't know why I was blessed with the best parents; I certainly don't deserve y'all. Y'all could have looked at me in the fourth grade when I started ordering podcast equipment from Amazon and laughed at me. Y'all could have refused to drop everything and drive me to my speeches or interviews because, at age eleven, regardless of how mature I thought I was, a driver's license was still out of reach. Y'all could have ignored me when I said I had this crazy dream of doing campus Q&As just days after you watched my friend be assassinated doing the same. But y'all didn't. Every late-night drive back from a swing state to make it to my 8 a.m. class, every early wake-up to be on a morning show, and every random adventure in between: I'm thankful for the unconventional way I've gotten to make memories along the way with y'all and learn everything I know from y'all. Neither this book nor my career would have been possible without y'all being my rock through it all. I love y'all.

Thank you, Ainslee: The best sister ever who asks me the most random, off-the-wall questions that remind me how little your average teen knows about politics. Thank you for always making me laugh, helping me stay trendy and cultured, and being my pickleball partner.

Thank you, Granny, Paw Paw, and Papa Doug: My personal hype squad who never misses one of my TV hits and are always there with cookies or ice cream when I get to come home. I'm so thankful for the example y'all have set for me.

Thank you to my entire extended family: I don't know how y'all put up with me, but I'm thankful y'all do. Thank you for planning dinners around my TV or travel schedule, and for always being there for me along this wild ride.

Thank you to my friends: Whether it's back home or at college, I struck gold when God put the best friends possible in my life. Thank y'all for being understanding, flexible, and always ready to fight off a protester who interrupts dinner.

Thank y'all for walking with me as brothers and sisters in Christ, keeping me grounded, and making me laugh along the way.

Thank you, Auburn: This hasn't been the first year any of us expected for me, but thank you for letting me be a student at the best university in the country, keeping me safe, still staying up to date with homework and exams, and being a true home away from home and "family" like the billboard claims. War Eagle always!

Thank you to my prayer warriors: You all know who you are if I randomly and frantically text you with a hurdle we have to clear along the way. When God says He'll be there if two or more are gathered, He really meant it. The church community and mentors that God has opened doors for me to sit alongside, be poured into by, and do life with have been the biggest blessing. I've genuinely felt the power of prayer on the road this year more than ever, and y'all taking the time out of your day to pray for our safety and success means the world.

Thank you, Eldad Yaron: They don't make better publicists than you. You make me look good and help me get on everybody's TV screens. I'm so grateful for your humor to keep me sane and for our friendship along the way.

Thank you, Brian Elliott and the Premiere dream team: The best speaking bureau team in America. Working with y'all to get to speak across the country has been such a blessing, and we've had so much fun together. Thank y'all for everything big and small, whether it's booking flights or helping me speak to some of the coolest groups in America. Your attention to detail and friendship are a joy to partner with.

Thank you, Tom Dean: What a fun journey we've had. I'm proud to call you a true friend and the best literary agent in the business. Anybody else would have looked at me in 2023 and called me crazy for trying to write and publish a book before I graduated high school. You went to bat for me, believed in me, and brought *One Generation Away* to the bestseller's list. I'm thankful I didn't scare you off, and we get to keep working together. Two down, a lifetime of more books to go. Enjoy well-deserved rest and watch some Alabama football.

Thank you, Marcus Costantino: I appreciate your friendship, brother. I'm indebted to your work as my mentor and researcher on both this title and *One Generation Away*. Between classes and a social life while writing these books, the pesky citations and cool stats wouldn't have made it in without your help. You're the only person who makes Zoom calls fun. Let's golf soon!

Thank you, Kathryn Riggs and the entire Regnery and Skyhorse Publishing team: Y'all believed in me when nobody else did and have become like my second family. Getting to do this second book together was painless and a breeze because y'all are total pros. This book was so much fun, and I can't wait for the next one!

About the Author

Brilyn Hollyhand has emerged as a force to be reckoned with in American political commentary at a remarkably young age. Dubbed "the internet's youngest voice of reason," as a twenty-year-old college freshman, Brilyn has already made significant strides within the political landscape, primarily through his engagement with conservative politics and youth voter outreach.

Brilyn's venture into politics began at the age of eleven, when he founded both "The Truth Gazette" newsletter and *The Brilyn Hollyhand Show* podcast in the fourth grade in July 2017. By his teenage years, Brilyn had become a familiar face on national cable news networks including Fox News, CNN, ABC News, NewsNation, and Newsmax, where he provided his unique perspective on current events through the lens of Generation Z.

In 2024, Brilyn published his first book, *One Generation Away: Why Now Is the Time to Restore American Freedom*, which quickly became recognized as a rallying cry for young conservatives and debuted at #2 on an Amazon bestsellers list. His political activism did not stop at media and literature. Brilyn was appointed to chair the Republican National Committee's inaugural Youth Advisory Council and served during for the 2024 election cycle, a role he embraced to directly influence and expand the GOP's outreach to younger voters and work with Trump to achieve the greatest comeback in political history. In 2022, Brilyn earned the prestigious John Lewis National Youth Leadership Award from the National Secretaries of State Association. In 2023, he was named one of *LA Weekly's* "Top 10 Visionaries to Look Out For," highlighting his role as a political prodigy and an inspiration for young individuals. As the *New York Times* noted in an October 2025 profile, Brilyn Hollyhand has emerged as one of the most prominent young conservatives in America, seen by many as part of the next generation poised to carry forward Charlie Kirk's legacy.

Brilyn Hollyhand's journey from a fourth-grade podcast host to a nationally recognized political commentator and bestselling author illustrates a precocious understanding of politics, media, and the power of youth engagement. In his free time, you can find Brilyn on a golf course or at the lake with friends and family. Today, Brilyn still hosts his viral Gen Z commentary show, *The Brilyn Hollyhand Show*, that he started way back in elementary school, where he still boldy breaks down the day's top stories and gives his unique perspective live from his dorm, available on all major platforms. Brilyn is a freshman at Auburn University and was born and raised in Tuscaloosa, Alabama.

To keep up with Brilyn's hot takes and watch his viral show, follow him on social media, @BrilynHollyhand, or visit his website, BrilynHollyhand.com, to check out his books or ask him to speak at your next event!

Notes

Introduction

1. NX Media Watch, "Charlie Kirk: 'When People Stop Talking . . . ,'" YouTube, September 11, 2025, https://www.youtube.com/watch?v=A0irjRxaigc.
2. Ronald Reagan, "Farewell Address to the Nation," Ronald Reagan Presidential Library & Museum, January 11, 1989, https://www.reaganlibrary.gov/archives/speech/farewell-address-nation.
3. Charlie Kirk, quoted by Eric Burlison, "Charlie Kirk's Prophetic Warning: When Dialogue Dies, Violence Thrives," Blaze Media, September 26, 2025, https://www.theblaze.com/columns/opinion/charlie-kirks-prophetic-warning-when-dialogue-dies-violence-thrives.
4. Charlie Kirk via Turning Point USA, "A Life of Faith, a Legacy That Endures: Remembering Charlie Kirk," YouTube, September 11, 2025, YouTube, https://www.youtube.com/watch?v=K_C-mj4dS4k.
5. Rush Limbaugh, "Never Panic!," Facebook, October 6, 2023, https://www.facebook.com/RushLimbaugh/videos/never-panic/1368585967089523/.

Chapter 1

1. Thomas Jefferson, "First Inaugural Address," March, 4, 1801, Yale Law School's Lillian Goldman Law Library, https://avalon.law.yale.edu/19th_century/jefinau1.asp.

2. Mark Twain, *Man Is the Only Animal That Blushes . . . or Needs To* (Los Angeles: Stanyan Books, 1970), 6.
3. Martin Luther King Jr., "Letter from a Birmingham Jail [King, Jr.]," African Studies Center—University of Pennsylvania, April 16, 1963, https://www.africa.upenn.edu/Articles_Gen/Letter_Birmingham.html.
4. Ronald Reagan, "Inaugural Address at Public Ceremony," Ronald Reagan Presidential Library & Museum, January 5, 1967, https://www.reaganlibrary.gov/archives/speech/january-5-1967-inaugural-address-public-ceremony.
5. Danny Hakim, Ken Bensinger, and Eileen Sullivan, "'We'll See You at Your House': How Fear and Menace Are Transforming Politics," *New York Times*, May 19, 2024, https://www.nytimes.com/2024/05/19/us/politics/political-violence.html, accessed March 4, 2026.
6. "Methodology: NPR/PBS News/Marist Poll of 1,477 National Adults," Marist Poll, October 1, 2025, https://maristpoll.marist.edu/wp-content/uploads/2025/09/NPR_PBS-News_Marist-Poll_USA-NOS-and-Tables_R2202509291454.pdf.
7. Brilyn Hollyhand, *One Generation Away*, (New York: Regnery, 2024), xxiii–xxiv.
8. David J. Harris Jr., Facebook Post with image, January 8, 2026, https://www.facebook.com/DavidJHarrisJr/posts/1453740192991184/.
9. "Gender Dysphoria Diagnosis," American Psychiatric Association, https://www.psychiatry.org/psychiatrists/diversity/education/transgender-and-gender-nonconforming-patients/gender-dysphoria-diagnosis, last accessed January 31, 2026.
10. Sine Institute of Policy & Politics, "Reimagining Higher Education: Young Voices, New Visions," October 2025, https://www.american.edu/sine-institute/upload/2025-sine-survey-full-results-final-57-read-only.pdf.
11. Breanne Deppisch, "'We Won't Cower': Young Conservatives Build on Kirk Legacy with Nationwide Speaking Tour," Fox News, September 18, 2025, https://www.foxnews.com/politics/we-wont-cower-young-conservatives-build-kirk-legacy-nationwide-speaking-tour.

Chapter 2

1. Joshua Coleman and Will Johnson, "How Estrangement Has Become an Epidemic in America," *Time*, December 13, 2024, https://time.com/7201531/family-estrangement-us-politics-epidemic-essay/.

2. Often attributed to G. Michael Hopf's novel *Those Who Remain* (2016).
3. Amy K. Hall, "A Call to Faithfulness from Os Guinness," Stand to Reason, January 20, 2017, https://www.str.org/w/a-call-to-faithfulness-from-os-guinness.
4. Gary Ryan Blair, "Gandhi's Way," EverythingCounts.com, January 20, 2019, https://www.everythingcounts.com/gandhis-way/.
5. Margaret Thatcher, May 3, 1989, quoted in *Politico*, https://www.politico.com/story/2013/04/margaret-thatcher-quotes-from-a-life-in-politics-089742.
6. C. S. Lewis, *Mere Christianity*, (San Francisco: HarperOne, 2001), 82.
7. Mark Twain, *Man Is the Only Animal That Blushes . . . or Needs To* (Los Angeles: Stanyan Books, 1970), 35.
8. Brilyn Hollyhand, "It's Time for Trump to Pull $9B from Harvard," Human Events, April 10, 2025, https://humanevents.com/2025/04/10/brilyn-hollyhand-its-time-for-trump-to-pull-9b-from-harvard.
9. PRRI (Public Religion Research Institute), "A Political and Cultural Glimpse into America's Future: Generation Z's Views on Generational Change and the Challenges and Opportunities Ahead," PRRI Survey Reports, January 22, 2024, https://prri.org/research/generation-zs-views-on-generational-change-and-the-challenges-and-opportunities-ahead-a-political-and-cultural-glimpse-into-americas-future/.

Chapter 3

1. John F. Kennedy, "Commencement Address at American University," John F. Kennedy Presidential Library and Museum, June 10, 1963, https://www.jfklibrary.org/archives/other-resources/john-f-kennedy-speeches/american-university-19630610.
2. Christopher J. Scalia, "My Father's Relationship with Justice Ginsburg—'Best of Friends,'" American Enterprise Institute, September 21, 2020, https://www.aei.org/articles/my-fathers-relationship-with-justice-ginsburg-best-of-friends/.
3. Claire Goforth, "White Nationalist Nazi Nick Fuentes Is Back on Twitter," The New Republic, January 13, 2026, https://newrepublic.com/post/170149/white-nationalist-nazi-nick-fuentes-back-twitter.
4. Matt Galka, "Future of Democratic Party: Ocasio-Cortez May Consider 2028 Senate or Presidential Run," FOX Baltimore, September 19, 2025, https://foxbaltimore.com/news/nation-world/future-of-democratic-party-ocasio-cortez-may-consider-2028-senate-or-presidential-demoratic-socialist-democratic-hakeem-jeffries-woke-dei.

5. Donald J. Trump (@realDonaldTrump), Truth Social post, November 10, 2025, https://truthsocial.com/@realDonaldTrump/115525636532373104.
6. Emily A. Vogels, "A Growing Share of Americans Are Familiar with 'Cancel Culture'," Pew Research Center—Short Reads, June 9, 2022, https://www.pewresearch.org/short-reads/2022/06/09/a-growing-share-of-americans-are-familiar-with-cancel-culture/.
7. Justine Coleman, "Poll: Plurality of Voters Say 'Cancel Culture' Has 'Gone Too Far,'" The Hill, July 22, 2020, https://thehill.com/homenews/news/508527-poll-plurality-of-voters-say-cancel-culture-has-gone-too-far/.
8. Ibid.
9. "RNC Announces Fox Business Republican Primary Debate with Partners Reagan Foundation, Univision, and Rumble," Ronald Reagan Presidential Foundation & Institute press release, August 9, 2023, https://www.reaganfoundation.org/about-us/press-releases/rnc-announces-fox-business-republican-primary-debate-with-partners-reagan-foundation-univision-and-rumble.
10. Mark Twain, *Man Is the Only Animal That Blushes . . . or Needs to* (Los Angeles: Stanyan Books, 1970), 12.

Chapter 4

1. Annalisa Wilson, "Disagreement Is Not Dangerous: The Lesson Charlie Kirk Leaves Behind," *Chicago Star*, September 25, 2025, https://www.chicagostarmedia.com/opinion/disagreement-is-not-dangerous-the-lesson-charlie-kirk-leaves-behind/article_6d30abc1-108f-4a17-b21c-9cf17c97a23e.html.
2. Dan Pilat and Dr. Sekoul Krastev, "Milton Friedman," The Decision Lab, https://thedecisionlab.com/thinkers/economics/milton-friedman, last accessed January 31, 2026.
3. S. M. Mehedi Zaman and Kiran Garimella, "Disagreement Is Disappearing on U.S. Cable Debate Shows," arXiv, November 19, 2025, https://arxiv.org/html/2511.15774v1, last accessed January 31, 2026.
4. Sophia Cai, "Trump Bombs the Bronx," Axios, May 24, 2024, https://www.axios.com/2024/05/24/trump-south.
5. Jo Ann Liguori, "20 Common Words That Used to Mean Completely Different Things," *Reader's Digest*, July 31, 2025, https://www.rd.com/list/words-changed-meaning/.
6. Mark Twain, *Man Is the Only Animal That Blushes . . . or Needs to*, (Los Angeles: Stanyan Books, 1970), 7.

7. Dennis Prager, "The Left has repeatedly refused to debate both Dennis and Charlie Kirk. Dennis calls them 'cowards,'" From *The Dennis Prager Show*, September 22, 2025, https://www.facebook.com/watch/?v=812061954682582.
8. C. S. Lewis, *Mere Christianity* (San Francisco: HarperCollins, 2001), 85.
9. Lewis, *Mere Christianity*, 87.
10. Ibid., 85.
11. Russel D. Moore, *Tempted and Tried: Temptation and the Triumphant of Christ* (Wheaton: Crossway, 2011), 20–21.
12. Tyler Staton, *Searching for Enough: The High-Wire Walk Between Doubt and Faith* (Grand Rapids: Zondervan, 2021), 46.

Chapter 5

1. Patrick Henry, "Virginia Convention Speech," March 23, 1775.
2. Thomas Paine, from *The American Crisis*, quoted in *The Patriots Reference* (Nashville: Thomas Nelson, 2014), 136.
3. Eric Metaxas, *Letter to the American Church* (Salem Books, 2022), Chapter 11, Chapter 7, Kindle Edition.
4. Jacob Bliss, "Exclusive: RNC Hopes to Attract Young Voters Ahead of 2024 by Launching 'Youth Advisory Council,'" Breitbart, May 9, 2023, https://www.breitbart.com/politics/2023/05/09/exclusive-rnc-hopes-to-attract-young-voters-ahead-2024-launching-youth-advisory-council/.
5. Gwen Ifill, "The 1992 Campaign: Youth Vote; Clinton Goes Eye to Eye With MTV Generation," *New York Times*, June 17, 1992, https://www.nytimes.com/1992/06/17/us/the-1992-campaign-youth-vote-clinton-goes-eye-to-eye-with-mtv-generation.
6. Dylan Wells, "RNC TikTok Influencers and Trump Delegates Collide in Youth Outreach Strategy," *Washington Post*, July 13, 2024, https://www.washingtonpost.com/politics/2024/07/13/rnc-tiktok-influencers-trump-delegates/.
7. Tufts CIRCLE, "Overall Youth Turnout Down From 2020 But Strong in Battleground States," Tufts University CIRCLE, November 7, 2024, https://circle.tufts.edu/latest-research/overall-youth-turnout-down-2020-strong-battleground-states.
8. "How Groups Voted in 2024," Roper Center for Public Opinion Research, https://ropercenter.cornell.edu/how-groups-voted-2024, last accessed January 31, 2026.
9. Ronald Reagan, "Inaugural Address," Ronald Reagan Presidential Library and Museum, January 5, 1967, https://www.reaganlibrary.gov/archives/speech/january-5-1967-inaugural-address-public-ceremony.

10. Ronald Reagan, "Address to the Nation on the Explosion of the Space Shuttle Challenger," Ronald Reagan Presidential Library & Museum, January 28, 1986, https://www.reaganlibrary.gov/archives/speech/address-nation-explosion-space-shuttle-challenger.
11. Samuel J. Abrams, "Gen Z Is Anything but Politically Ill-Informed," American Council of Trustees and Alumni, April 7, 2021, https://www.goacta.org/news-item/gen-z-is-anything-but-politically-ill-informed/#:~:text=Despite%20high%20voter%20turnout%2C%20countless,Z%20is%20not%20an%20outlier.
12. Abby Kiesa, Ruby Belle Booth, Noorya Hayat, Kei Kawashima-Ginsberg, and Alberto Medina, "Growing Voters Report," Tufts CIRCLE, May 2024, https://circle.tufts.edu/sites/default/files/2024-05/circle_growing_voters_report.pdf.
13. Michelle Faverio and Olivia Sidoti, "Teens, Social Media and Technology 2024," Pew Research Center, December 12, 2024, https://www.pewresearch.org/internet/2024/12/12/teens-social-media-and-technology-2024/.

Chapter 6

1. Eleanor Roosevelt, "If You Ask Me," Columbian College of Arts & Sciences, September 1944, https://erpapers.columbian.gwu.edu/quotations-eleanor-roosevelt?utm_source=chatgpt.com.
2. Centers for Disease Control and Prevention, "Mental Health," CDC Healthy Youth, November 29, 2024, https://www.cdc.gov/healthy-youth/mental-health/.
3. The Jed Foundation, "Mental Health and Suicide Statistics," https://jedfoundation.org/mental-health-and-suicide-statistics/, last accessed February 15, 2026.
4. CocaColaSuperbowl, "Coca-Cola Jinx," YouTube, January 31, 2008, https://www.youtube.com/watch?v=lHk7kYYroRU.
5. CharlieKirkSavage, "The Zohran Mamdani Movement Is a Distress Signal from Gen Z," YouTube, October 13, 2025, https://www.youtube.com/shorts/mzP-mQQWPB0.
6. Jonathan J. Cooper, "What Americans Think about Socialism and Capitalism, According to a New Gallup Poll," The Associated Press, September 8, 2025, https://www.ap.org/news-highlights/spotlights/2025/what-americans-think-about-socialism-and-capitalism-according-to-a-new-gallup-poll/.
7. Erica Pandey and Margaret Talev, "Poll: College Students Prefer Socialism to Capitalism," Axios, November 1, 2025, https://www.axios.com/2025/11/01/socialism-capitalism-college-voters.

8. Margaret Thatcher's widely acknowledged comment, quoted by Lawrence W. Reed, "Margaret Thatcher on Socialism: 20 of Her Best Quotes," Foundation for Economic Education, February 8, 2020, https://fee.org/articles/margaret-thatcher-on-socialism-20-of-her-best-quotes/.
9. "Cyberbullying Data," Cyberbullying Research Center, February 16, 2024, https://cyberbullying.org/2023-cyberbullying-data.
10. Robert Shibley, "2026 College Free Speech Rankings," Foundation for Individual Rights and Expression (FIRE), 2026, https://www.thefire.org/research-learn/2026-college-free-speech-rankings.
11. John F. Kennedy, "Address Before the American Newspaper Publishers Association," John F. Kennedy Presidential Library and Museum, April 27, 1961, https://www.jfklibrary.org/archives/other-resources/john-f-kennedy-speeches/american-newspaper-publishers-association-19610427.
12. Andrew Peterson, "Christian Faith, the Arts, and Imagination" resources page, C. S. Lewis Institute, June 18, 2021, https://www.cslewisinstitute.org/resources/christian-faith-the-arts-and-imagination/.

Chapter 7

1. Richard Nixon, *In The Arena: A Memoir of Victory, Defeat, and Renewal* (New York: Simon & Schuster, Kindle Edition, 1990), 222.
2. G. K Chesterton, *Illustrated London News*, 1925, quoted by The Catholic Thing, January 29, 2016, https://www.thecatholicthing.org/2016/01/29/chesterton-on-progressives-and-conservatives/.
3. Kendall Tietz, "UNC Frat Members Who Protected American Flag Recount Chaotic Protest That 'Blew My Mind,'" Fox News, May 7, 2024, https://www.foxnews.com/media/unc-frat-members-protected-american-flag-recount-chaotic-protest-blew-my-mind.
4. Acton Institute, "Justice Antonin Scalia," author profile, https://www.acton.org/about/author/justice-antonin-scalia, last accessed February 15, 2026.
5. George Barna, "104 Million People of Faith, Including 32 Million Christian Regular Churchgoers, Projected to Abstain from Voting in November," George Barna, October 10, 2024, https://georgebarna.com/2024/10/104-million-people-of-faithincluding-32-million-christian-regular-churchgoersprojected-to-abstain-from-voting-in-november/.
6. Elie Wiesel, "Nobel Peace Prize 1986 Acceptance Speech," The Nobel Prize, December 10, 1986, https://www.nobelprize.org/prizes/peace/1986/wiesel/acceptance-speech/.

7. Doug Hershey, "Silence in Face of Evil: Bonhoeffer and Antisemitism," Israel Today, January 21, 2016, https://firmisrael.org/learn/silence-in-face-of-evil-bonhoeffer-and-antisemitism/.
8. Jessica Theodule and Jeb Bell, "Insight Report III: Already Report Encountering Fake Election News," Project Liberty Institute, June 11, 2024, https://www.projectliberty.io/insight-report-iii/#:~:text=Widespread%20concern%20about%20fake%20election,or%20incorrect%20was%20actually%20true.
9. Elisa Shearer, Michael Lipka, Sarah Naseer, Emily Tomasik, and Mark Jurkowitz, "How Closely Are Americans Following Election News, and What Are They Seeing?" Pew Research Center, October 10, 2024, https://www.pewresearch.org/journalism/2024/10/10/how-closely-are-americans-following-election-news-and-what-are-they-seeing/.
10. "It Is Not the Critic Who Counts," from a speech at the Sorbonne, Paris, on April 23, 1910, Theodore Roosevelt Conservation Partnership, https://www.trcp.org/2011/01/18/it-is-not-the-critic-who-counts/.
11. Lee Edwards, PhD, "Standing Athwart History: The Political Thought of William F. Buckley Jr.," The Heritage Foundation, May 5, 2010, https://www.heritage.org/political-process/report/standing-athwart-history-the-political-thought-william-f-buckley-jr.
12. Jerry Seinfeld, *Seinfeld*, Quote from Season 4, Episode 23, https://seinfeldism.com/seinfeld-quote.php?id=2447.
13. David Montgomery, "What Americans really think about political violence," September 12, 2025, YouGov, https://today.yougov.com/politics/articles/52960-charlie-kirk-americans-political-violence-poll.
14. W. A. Criswell, "Whether We Live or Die," sermon delivered at the Southern Baptist Convention Pastors' Conference, Dallas, Texas, 1985, https://wacriswell.com/sermons/1985/whether-we-live-or-die-sbc/.

Chapter 8

1. Abraham Lincoln, "Second Inaugural Address of Abraham Lincoln," March 4, 1865, Yale Law School Lillian Goldman Law Library, https://avalon.law.yale.edu/19th_century/lincoln2.asp.
2. C. S. Lewis, *Mere Christianity* (San Francisco: HarperOne, 2001), 72.
3. Eric W. Dolan, "Extremism and Attention: Radical Views Are Rewarded on Social Media, New Research Reveals," PsyPost, April 16, 2024, https://www.psypost.org/extremism-and-attention-radical-views-are-rewarded-on-social-media-new-research-reveals/.

4. Justin Taylor, "How Much Do You Have to Hate Somebody to Not Proselytize?," The Gospel Coalition, November 18, 2009, https://www.thegospelcoalition.org/blogs/justin-taylor/how-much-do-you-have-to-hate-somebody-to-not-proselytize/.
5. Mark Twain, *Man Is the Only Animal That Blushes . . . or Needs To* (Los Angeles: Stanyan Books, 1970), 1.
6. "Top 10 Obama Backlash Moments: Beer Summit Gone Wrong," *Time*, https://content.time.com/time/specials/packages/article/0,28804,1929415_1929418_1929404,00.html, last accessed January 31, 2026.
7. Nick Freitas, "Do What We Want or Else You're Racist," Facebook, https://www.facebook.com/reel/1002450448415398, last accessed March 1, 2026.

Chapter 9

1. Ronald Reagan, quote from remarks honoring Nancy Reagan at the Republican National Convention on August 15, 1988, Reagan Presidential Foundation & Institute, https://www.reaganfoundation.org/ronald-reagan/quotes/when-our-children-turn-the-pages-of-our-lives-i-hope.
2. Donald J. Trump, "Commencement Remarks at the University of Alabama," C-SPAN, May 1, 2025, https://www.c-span.org/program/white-house-event/president-trump-commencement-remarks-at-university-of-alabama/659364.
3. "'Gen Z Is MORE Conservative Than You Think,' Brilyn Hollyhand DROPS DEVASTATING TRUTH For Democrats!," *The Officer Tatum Show*, October 24, 2025, https://www.youtube.com/watch?v=3KrrqWi6IlY.
4. Alberto Medina, Sara Suzuki, and Ruby Belle Booth, "Young Voters Power Mamdani Victory, Shape Key 2025 Elections," Tufts CIRCLE, November 5, 2025, https://circle.tufts.edu/latest-research/young-voters-power-mamdani-victory-shape-key-2025-elections.
5. Adeola Adeosum, "Democratic Pollster 'Shocked' At Gen Z's Conservative Shift," *Newsweek*, March 22, 2025, https://www.newsweek.com/democratic-pollster-shocked-gen-z-conservative-shift-2049107.
6. Tufts CIRCLE, "The Youth Vote in 2024," Tufts University CIRCLE (2025), https://circle.tufts.edu/2024-election, last accessed January 31, 2026.
7. Breanne Deppisch, "'We Won't Cower': Young Conservatives Build on Kirk Legacy with Nationwide Speaking Tour," Fox News, September 18, 2025, https://www.foxnews.com/politics/we-wont-cower-young-conservatives-build-kirk-legacy-nationwide-speaking-tour.

8. Mark Twain, *Man Is the Only Animal That Blushes . . . or Needs to* (Los Angeles: Stanyan Books, 1970), 2.
9. Mark Twain, *Man Is the Only Animal That Blushes . . . or Needs to* (Los Angeles: Stanyan Books, 1970), 42.
10. *Landman*, "Ainsley Meets Her Roommate," Landman Official, YouTube, January 16, 2026, https://www.youtube.com/watch?v=ryIeOxe9lBw.

Conclusion

1. Ronald Reagan, "Farewell Address to the Nation," January 11, 1989, Reagan Foundation, https://www.reaganfoundation.org/ronald-reagan/speeches/farewell-address-to-the-nation.
2. Samuel J. Abrams, "America's Third Places Are Disappearing and Why It Matters," American Enterprise Institute, December 2, 2025, https://www.aei.org/society-and-culture/americas-third-places-are-disappearing-and-why-it-matters/.
3. "Three in Four Families Use Phones at Dinner Table, Says Survey," BBC, May 2, 2025, https://www.bbc.co.uk/newsround/articles/cvgpy6zxpz0o.
4. JD Vance, "Vice President JD Vance Delivers Remarks at Turning Point USA's America Fest," The White House, YouTube, December 21, 2025, https://www.youtube.com/watch?v=e8uvILQ8WiM&t.
5. "The Benefits of the Family Table," American College of Pediatrics, February 2021, https://acpeds.org/wp-content/uploads/2025/04/The-Benefits-of-the-Family-Table-2.2021-1.pdf.
6. Ibid.
7. Mark Twain, *Man Is the Only Animal That Blushes . . . or Needs To* (Los Angeles: Stanyan Books, 1970), 23.
8. Noah Sheidlower and Juliana Kaplan, "Forget Swing States. Here's How the Generations Flipped on Election Day," Yahoo News, November 9, 2024, https://www.yahoo.com/news/forget-swing-states-heres-generations-090002363.html.